STOCK IN TRADE

A Guide
to the World
and Work of
Wall Street

Securities Industry Association

Dearborn
Financial Publishing, Inc.

While a great deal of care has been taken to provide accurate and current information, the ideas, suggestions, general principles and conclusions presented in this text are subject to local, state and federal laws and regulations, court cases and any revisions of same. The reader is thus urged to consult legal counsel regarding any points of law—this publication should not be used as a substitute for competent legal advice.

Executive Editor: Kimberly K. Walker-Daniels
Development Editor: Nicola Bell
Cover Design: Vito dePinto

© 1992 by Dearborn Financial Publishing, Inc.
Published by Dearborn Financial Publishing, Inc.

Printed in the United States of America.

92 93 94   10 9 8 7 6 5 4 3 2 1

Library of Congress Cataloging-in-Publication Data

Stock in trade : a guide to the world and work of Wall Street /
   [executive editor, Kimberly K. Walker-Daniels]
      p.   cm.
   "Produced ... in cooperation with the Securities Industry
Association."
   Includes index.
   ISBN 0-7931-0356-8
   1. Securities industry—United States. I. Walker-Daniels,
Kimberly K.   II. Securities Industry Association.
HG4910.S687   1992
332.63'2—dc20   91-42534
                                                 CIP
                                                 Rev

Contents

Chapter 5   Trading Securities

Chapter 6   Securities Regulation

Chapter 9   Economics, Analysis and the Securities Industry

Foreword

The securities industry in the United States, often referred to as "Wall Street," is a thriving, challenging workplace for hundreds of thousands of men and women.

Those who work within our industry contribute directly or indirectly to our two basic missions:

- Providing the capital needed by business enterprises as well as by units of government at the local, state and federal levels ... capital that fuels our economy and fosters the creation of jobs.
- Providing advice and other investment services to individuals and institutions ... services that help Americans to enhance their standard of living and meet their financial needs, including education, housing, health and retirement.

The purpose of this text is to introduce you to the securities industry. Whether you are already a part of our industry, a student, someone interested in a career in this business or someone who simply wishes to know what Wall Street is all about, you will find this book of great value.

Edward I. O'Brien
President
Securities Industry Association

Acknowledgments

The Securities Industry Association and Dearborn Financial Publishing, Inc. express appreciation to the following individuals for their invaluable assistance in the development of this text:

Donnis Casey (A.G. Edwards & Sons, Inc.); Joni Cleary and Robert K. Pearce (Edward D. Jones & Co.); Michael Cunningham and Judy Bleemer (Dean Witter Reynolds, Inc.); John Donnelly (Smith Barney, Harris Upham & Co., Incorporated); Bruce S. Foerster (Lehman Brothers); Gloria Gibson (Interstate/Johnson Lane Corporation); Thomas F. Lee, Jr. (Donaldson, Lufkin & Jenrette Securities Corporation); Benjamin L. Lubin (Securities Industry Management Corp.); Vincent Morano (John Hancock Clearing Corp.); Joyce Murter and William T. Smoot (Alex. Brown & Sons Incorporated); David Nelson (Raymond James Financial, Inc.); Allan H. Pessin (consultant to the securities industry); Catherine C. Stratford (Wheat, First Securities, Inc.); and LuAnne Waltemath (J.C. Bradford & Co.).

Appreciation is also extended to Mark Emmons, Kimberly K. Walker-Daniels and Nicola Bell, who led this project at Dearborn Publishing, as well as to Adrian L. Banky and Jack O'Neill, who directed this effort on behalf of the Securities Industry Association.

Chapter 1

Evolution of the Securities Industry

"Capital is to the progress of society what gas is to a car."

James Truslow Adams

Overview

The securities industry is a complex, constantly changing, living, breathing, growing entity that employs hundreds of thousands of people. This book is intended to provide you with an overview of this industry, the people who work in it and the businesses that compose it.

Crucial to understanding the way investments and securities work is a knowledge of their history and origins. This chapter focuses on the evolution of money, the origin of tradable securities and the firms and exchanges that make securities trading possible.

□ THE ORIGIN OF MONEY

The origin of modern money can be traced to the beginnings of an economy based on trade. Initially, all trading was accomplished through barter. As an example, if a person had an extra cow and needed a spinning wheel, he would trade the cow to someone who needed a cow and who had an extra spinning wheel. One drawback to barter is that you have to locate someone who has what you want and wants what you have. A second drawback is that you have to carry your extra goods around with you in order to be ready to trade. If you do not have your goods ready to trade, you could miss the opportunity to exchange something you have for something you need.

As the drawbacks to barter as a means of redistributing goods became evident, societies moved toward developing a more efficient means of taking care of the inequities of supply and demand. It was recognized early on that some commonly accepted medium of exchange was necessary—an item of recognized value that was easy to carry, durable, universally accepted and divisible into smaller units. Those mediums of exchange that met these requirements represented the earliest money.

In the early years of man's economic development, currency took many forms—wood, stone, pottery, shells, beads, animal hides and teeth or precious metals, among others. While various forms of currency have been placed in use over the course of history, none has proved as useful as the precious metals copper, silver, gold and platinum. These precious metals met all of the requirements of currency and offered an added attraction—they were relatively rare and therefore came to have a value independent of the value of the goods for which they could be traded.

Eventually, even coins made of precious metals became cumbersome. Coins can be heavy to carry and are subject to both loss and theft. As an alternative to dealing in metal coins, people who entered into transactions for large amounts of money began issuing *receipts* representing those coins. These receipts (or *notes*) could then be redeemed in gold by the holder at a later date. Notes represented the beginnings of paper currency.

Paper currency, while offering solutions to many of the problems of coins, had its own shortcomings. Every monarch, landowner and merchant was free to issue his own notes, and society saw a proliferation of types, denominations, marketability and values. In time, local and national governments took over the responsibility of issuing currency and over the years standardized it and made it easier to use.

For many years, these official currencies continued to be redeemable for a specific amount of gold. Then, during the period between World War I and World War II, the governments of most modern nations discontinued the practice of redeeming currency with gold. Governments declared that it was no longer necessary to back the paper money they issued with gold, and that the paper notes themselves represented **legal tender**. The paper money circulating in each nation was accepted by its citizens as official currency, and its value was based on the government's ability to maintain its economy's health and the money's economic value.

☐ THE ORIGIN OF SECURITIES

As currency developed over time, people began to use money not only to trade for goods, but also as a means of storing, measuring and accumulating wealth. Those with excess stores of money (which represented early examples of **disposable income**) began to look for ways to use that money.

As people's basic needs for food, clothing and shelter were satisfied, they began to experiment with ways in which money could be made to produce more wealth. That is, people sought ways to put their money to work for them.

Some people discovered excess money could be used to buy goods at one price and sell them for a higher price, resulting in a profit to the trader. Others learned that excess money could be loaned to people who needed money, and that these borrowers were often willing to pay for the privilege of borrowing—that is, lending excess money to someone who needed it could generate interest. So was born the concept of investment capital—money available for economic purposes other than trade.

In these early ventures into using money to generate more money, the parties involved often drew up a contract (often referred to as a *note*) to record the particulars of an agreement. As an example, a contract could serve as a record of the fact that one individual intended to borrow money from another and promised to repay it at a future date. The lender would hold the note until the borrower repaid the amount borrowed. Today's banking system still relies on the simple promissory note as the basis for many of its loans.

Contracts were also used to represent agreements between parties to split the cost of running a business. In many instances, one or more partners in a business venture agreed to put up the majority of the money, and the other partners agreed to run the business. Each owned a share of the business in return for contributing what he could—money or knowledge and expertise.

As a means of safeguarding the interests of all parties to these financial transactions, the details of these early ventures were duly recorded on paper in the form of an agreement or a contract. The written records of these financial transactions were the predecessors of the first securities.

Pooled capital. The practice of many individuals pooling their capital and sharing in the ownership of a single asset probably originated with the great tea merchant ships of the 15th and 16th century. The cost of sending a single ship from England to India was great, and only members of the ruling class and the wealthiest of individuals could afford to sponsor them. If, as happened frequently, the ship sank, the entire fortune of the lone sponsor could sink with it.

The risks of investing all of one's assets in a single venture such as a merchant ship were great, but the return on an investment in a ship and its cargo could be even greater. Because of the high level of risks involved, investors began to search for ways to spread out and lessen these risks. Soon, many merchants with investment capital began pooling their money and using those pooled funds to invest in several expeditions. By doing so, even if one ship, its crew and its cargo sank, the investors did not lose everything they had invested in the venture: the profits from the remaining ships would cover the costs of the one lost.

The physical assets of these shipping companies (the boats, cargo, equipment and so on) were often referred to as their *stock*. The shared ownership of these shipping companies came to be known as *shares* in the stock of the company.

Forms of Business Organization

Individual (or sole) proprietorship. A sole proprietor (or single owner) controls a business totally and makes all business decisions (hours of operation, activities, location, services offered and more). If for any reason the owner could not continue to operate the business, it probably would cease to exist. A sole proprietor is personally liable for all business debts (that is, she has unlimited liability), and any credit extended to the business is restricted to the sole proprietor's personal creditworthiness.

Corporation. Corporations have a continuous (and theoretically perpetual) life. Because its continued existence does not depend on one or more key individuals, a corporation will not disappear at the loss of an officer or a director. To establish itself as a corporation, a business must file a certificate of incorporation with the secretary of the state in which the company's official office is located. When accepted, this certificate becomes the corporate charter, describing the line of business the corporation will be in and giving authorization to the company to issue a certain number of shares of common stock. Corporations are able to raise large amounts of capital by selling stock to the public or by borrowing capital from investors through various debt offerings. A corporation's charter is subject to the laws of the state in which it is filed.

Corporations are the most common form of organization for businesses other than the very small, primarily because they offer their owners (the stockholders) limited liability. If a corporation goes into bankruptcy, creditors have recourse to the corporation's assets, but not to the assets of the stockholders. Stockholders are liable only to the extent of their individual investments. In addition, corporate ownership is easily transferred because ownership of the corporation is represented by shares of stock, and transferring ownership can be accomplished by instructing a broker to buy or sell those shares.

There are several disadvantages to the corporate form of business. Formation can be complicated and costly, running from hundreds to millions of dollars. Differences in state statutes often make it difficult to transact business in states other than the state in which the company was incorporated. In addition, corporations are subject to strict government control and supervision and are heavily taxed. Corporate earnings are subject to double taxation: a corporation first pays the corporate income tax and then investors pay taxes on dividends distributed to them by the corporation.

Partnerships and Limited Partnerships

Partnerships consist of two or more individuals who own the business, either in equal or differing percentage interests.

Partnerships are similar to sole proprietorships in the sense that each general partner has unlimited liability for the obligations of the partnership. For example, if a partnership is in default on a loan, the creditor may seek repayment from the personal assets of the general partners. Partnerships are also similar to sole proprietorships in terms of taxation; that is, partnership profits are allocated to the partners and then taxed once, rather than twice as is the case with the corporate form of ownership. However, unlike a sole proprietorship, a partnership is able to look beyond one individual for the ownership capital needed to start and operate the business.

A **limited partnership** is a form of partnership that enables individuals to *limit* their liability to their investment in the business. In the securities industry, this form of ownership is often used for **direct participation programs (DPPs)**, such as investments in real estate or in oil or gas development. A DPP typically is owned by a general partner along with a number of limited partners. A DPP pays no dividends, but passes income, gains, losses, deductions and credits directly to the investors.

□ THE ORIGIN OF SECURITIES MARKETS

People who owned securities (such as equity in tea ships or interest in promissory notes) often found that they needed to convert these assets into hard cash before the agreement was scheduled to conclude (that is, before the ships returned or before the notes were due). They quickly discovered that even though these assets had value, finding someone to buy the assets from them when they needed to raise cash quickly could be very difficult. Conversely, people who had excess cash and wanted to put money into equities or promissory notes often had trouble finding such investment opportunities. What was needed was some place and means by which people interested in selling their investments for cash could meet with people who had cash they wanted to invest.

As financial instruments such as shares of stock and notes of indebtedness became more common, some businessmen began to meet regularly to buy and sell them. In the United States, these meetings were often held in the coffeehouses and out in the open on the streets of major centers of business such as Philadelphia, Boston and New York City. People who were interested in buying or selling a security would come to the street meeting place when they knew others were going to be there and announce their wish to buy or sell. If someone in the crowd on the street was interested in what the person had to offer, a deal could be struck. On occasion, more than one person might be interested in buying or selling the security and a shouting match would take place, with each participant trying to cry out a better price or better terms than his competitors. These *open outcry* auctions (also known as *double auctions* because both the buyers and the sellers are competing against each other for the best price) are still very much in evidence today in the trading methods employed by stock exchanges.

While the trading of securities was becoming easier and more commonplace, it was still the province of the merchants and the wealthy, and would remain so for some years. In 1789, the U.S. Congress authorized the first U.S. government bond issue to pay for the War of Independence. Less than two years later, the Secretary of the Treasury authorized the sale of stock in the newly formed Bank of the United States. Before the end of 1790, the first stock exchange in the Western hemisphere was formed in Philadelphia to trade the new bank stocks and government bonds. By 1792, another group of businessmen and merchants had begun to meet in New York to conduct public auctions of bank stocks, government bonds and the securities of other fledgling U.S. corporations. Their chosen meeting place was underneath a buttonwood tree on Wall Street in New York City, long a center of trading and commerce, only a few yards from where the New York Stock Exchange (the NYSE) stands today. Other national and regional stock exchanges (such as the American, Midwest, Boston, Cincinnati and Pacific) followed.

As the economy of the United States grew, so did the new exchanges, each evolving to meet the special needs of its clientele. Within a few years, the traders at the Philadelphia Stock Exchange had expanded into assisting other merchants and new businesses to raise capital through issuing stocks and bonds. The traders at the New York Stock Exchange traded primarily in the shares of large, well-established national companies. The American Stock Exchange (the AMEX or Curb Exchange) began as the New York Curb Market Association in 1911, named after the curb on William Street on which many early trades took place. Traders at the American Stock Exchange concentrated primarily on the stocks of new and small- to medium-size companies, particularly those involved in exploiting the resources of the new nation. Today, many mid-size companies and oil and gas company stocks still find their primary market on the American Stock Exchange.

As the public markets for securities grew through the 1800s and 1900s, many new companies took advantage of the growing ease with which capital could be raised through the public issuance of stocks and bonds. As a means of exerting some form of control over these newly issued securities, the two largest American exchanges, the NYSE and the AMEX, set requirements for securities they were willing to let their members trade on their premises and developed lists of those securities. The exchanges set minimum standards for company size, earnings and number of available shares (among other things) necessary to qualify for the listing. A great many companies were not eligible for the NYSE and AMEX listings because they were too small or did not have the required revenue, stockholder or income base. Some companies chose not to incur the expense or the ongoing reporting processes incident to exchange listing.

Even though the securities of these other companies were not listed on either of these exchanges, there still existed a need for a marketplace through which their securities could be traded. To meet this need, an **over-the-counter (OTC) market** developed to facilitate trading in these unlisted securities.

In the early years, this OTC market formed an indirect link between customers and the brokerage firms that had formed to carry on the business of trading securities. Customers who wanted to sell securities could bring them to the front counter of a brokerage firm and the brokers representing the firm would make a bid for them. Customers who wanted to buy securities would bring their money to the counter, and the brokers would look through their books to learn what securities were available for sale at what prices. This OTC market has since developed into an extensive, international, computerized network of brokers trading in a wide range of unlisted securities.

In 1939, the **National Association of Securities Dealers (NASD)** was formed. Its members gave the NASD the right to regulate them, to oversee the trading of all listed and unlisted securities and to provide a formal market for over-the-counter trades. In 1971, the NASD launched the **National Association of Securities Dealers Automated Quotation (NASDAQ)** stock market, which has become the second largest equity market in the United States and the third largest in the world. The NASD regulates NASDAQ and the rest of the OTC market. In 1975, the **Municipal Securities Rulemaking Board (MSRB)** was formed to make rules regarding the issuance and trading of municipal securities.

□ INTERNATIONAL EXCHANGES

As securities markets developed in the United States, they developed in many other nations as well. More than 140 stock, option and commodities exchanges exist in the world today. Among the largest stock exchanges in the world in 1991 (ranked by share value traded) were:

		$ Millions
1.	USA (all exchanges)	2,254,983
2.	Japan	995,939
3.	Frankfurt	409,301
4.	Taiwan	365,232
5.	London	317,866
6.	Paris	118,218
7.	Korea	85,464
8.	Toronto	78,160
9.	Amsterdam	76,974
10.	Zurich	68,836
11.	Sydney	46,835
12.	Milan	43,307

The locations of the world's largest stock exchanges are shown in Figure 1.

Most free-market countries have national exchanges, and some have regional markets. Although they all are in the business of buying and selling securities, customs and practices differ widely. The role of the participants, the ways they are managed and the regulation of the

FIGURE 1   The Major Stock Exchanges of the World

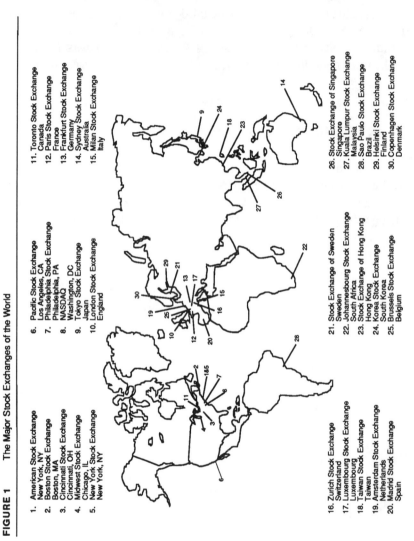

1. American Stock Exchange
   New York, NY
2. Boston Stock Exchange
   Boston, MA
3. Cincinnati Stock Exchange
   Cincinnati, OH
4. Midwest Stock Exchange
   Chicago, IL
5. New York Stock Exchange
   New York, NY

6. Pacific Stock Exchange
   Los Angeles, CA
7. Philadelphia Stock Exchange
   Philadelphia, PA
8. NASDAQ
   Washington, DC
9. Tokyo Stock Exchange
   Japan
10. London Stock Exchange
    England

11. Toronto Stock Exchange
    Canada
12. Paris Stock Exchange
    France
13. Frankfurt Stock Exchange
    Germany
14. Sydney Stock Exchange
    Australia
15. Milan Stock Exchange
    Italy

16. Zurich Stock Exchange
    Switzerland
17. Luxembourg Stock Exchange
    Luxembourg
18. Taiwan Stock Exchange
    Taiwan
19. Amsterdam Stock Exchange
    Netherlands
20. Madrid Stock Exchange
    Spain

21. Stock Exchange of Sweden
    Sweden
22. Johannesbourg Stock Exchange
    South Africa
23. Stock Exchange of Hong Kong
    Hong Kong
24. Korea Stock Exchange
    South Korea
25. Brussels Stock Exchange
    Belgium

26. Stock Exchange of Singapore
    Singapore
27. Kuala Lumpur Stock Exchange
    Malaysia
28. Sao Paulo Stock Exchange
    Brazil
29. Helsinki Stock Exchange
    Finland
30. Copenhagen Stock Exchange
    Denmark

exchanges vary from country to country, but all of the exchanges are dedicated to ensuring that those who have capital to invest can trade fairly with those who have investments that they wish to sell.

In the following chapters, you will find an overview of the various elements of the modern securities industry and their impact. We will also look at the individual roles of the people involved in this industry and how these roles relate to the brokerage firm, the regulatory environment and the modern marketplace.

☐ SUMMARY

This chapter laid the basis for the discussions in all of the chapters to come. Now that we have introduced the origins of money, securities and the markets, and the different types of business organizations, their advantages and disadvantages, you will be able to develop a better understanding of the products, markets, businesses and people we will be introducing throughout the remainder of this book.

In the following chapters, we will explore each of these topics in more depth and will show you how the parts of the industry interrelate to form a cohesive, efficient industry.

□ REVIEW

Check how well you have learned the information contained in this chapter by completing the following sentences.

One of man's earliest methods of trading goods he had for goods he needed was known as

_____

(See page 2)

Money that is available for economic purposes other than trade is known as

_____

(See page 3)

The first stock exchange in the Western hemisphere was formed in

_____

(See page 7)

Securities that are not listed on any exchange are traded in the

_____

(See page 8)

An early trading method that is still used on the floors of stock exchanges is the

_____

(See page 7)

Chapter 2

Equity, Debt and Special Securities

"... the market is remarkably efficient at properly reflecting the true worth of a company."

Robert L. Hagin

Overview

With the evolution of money and the means to create, hold and increase investable wealth, the number and types of investments available have evolved as well. Most investments can be divided into two general categories—ownership interests (also known as *equity investments*) and loan agreements (also known as *debt instruments*).

The best known of the equity investments in the securities industry are **common** and **preferred stock**. A share of stock represents a piece of ownership in the corporation that issued the stock. Stock rights, stock options, stock warrants, mutual fund shares and limited partnership units also represent forms of equity.

The best known of the debt instruments are **bonds** and **debentures**. Bills, notes, bankers' acceptances, commercial paper and certificates of deposit are all forms of debt. By investing in a bond, an investor agrees to lend money to a borrower (such as a corporation or government) in return for interest on that loan. At the end of an agreed-upon period of time, the borrower is obligated to repay the loan in full.

☐ EQUITY SECURITIES

The equity trading market is large, and getting larger virtually every year. In 1965, the market value of all equities outstanding in the United States was $714 billion. By 1991, this market had reached $4.4 trillion. In 1965, only 10% of all Americans owned equity securities. By 1990, just 25 years later, that figure had doubled to 21%. More and more Americans are looking at equity investing as a way to meet their financial goals.

Figure 2 shows a typical quotation of stock prices, representing a composite of prices as reported by various markets.

Common Stock

Shares of stock represent ownership (or equity) in a corporation. Companies issue stock as a primary means of raising business capital, and investors who buy those shares (either during the **initial public offering** or later, in the secondary market) are the owners of those companies. Whatever property a business owns (that is, its assets) less the claims of its creditors (its liabilities) belongs to the owners of the business, its stockholders.

A company can also issue bonds as a means of raising capital, but the bondholders are not considered owners of the corporation; they are considered lenders.

If a company issues 100 shares of common stock, each of those shares represents a 1% ownership of that company and may give its holder one vote in the company's management. A person who owns ten shares of stock would own 10% of the company (and may be entitled to ten votes) and so on. In today's business world, it is not unusual to see companies that have issued 1 million or more shares of common stock. Because each of these shares carries with it the same rights and privileges of every other share, it is easy to see how conflicts could arise regarding the management of these companies by their many rightful owners, the stockholders.

To avoid such potential management conflicts, most corporations are organized in such a way that the holders of their common stock regularly vote for and elect a limited number of people, generally between ten and twenty, to a board of directors to direct the company's business for them.

The board, in turn, oversees paid managers, who manage the company. By electing a board of directors, stockholders still have a say in the management of a company, but do not have to bother with the day-to-day details of its operations.

Investors buy common stock for several reasons. Common stock offers its owners the opportunity for capital growth (the price of the shares could rise in the market). Common stock offers investors some protection against inflation because companies' income and asset values tend to rise in times of rising prices. Common stock can also offer dividend income if the issuing company chooses to distribute some of its profits to its shareholders by declaring and paying a dividend.

Another advantage of equity investments is their limited liability. *Limited liability* means that all an investor has at risk is the value of his

---

FIGURE 2   Example of Stock Transactions as Reported by the NYSE

New York Stock Exchange Composite Transactions

Tuesday, September 13, 1998
Quotations include trades on the Midwest, Pacific, Philadelphia, Boston and Cincinnati Stock Exchanges and reported by the National Association of Securities Dealers and INSTINET.

52 Weeks High	Low	Stock	Div	Yld %	PE Ratio	Sales 100s	High	Low	Close	Net Chg.
80	40	ABCorp	.75	.1	12	3329	78	71	73	- 1 1/2
n 8 3/8	6 1/2	ACM IncFd	1.01	12.4	...	178	8 1/4	8 1/8	8 1/8	- 1/8
42 5/8	26 7/8	ALFA	2.40	5.6	12	x 1265	42 5/8	41 1/4	42 5/8	+1 1/4
35	24 5/8	Anchor	1.48	4.9	36	1960	30	29 3/4	30	+ 1/4
27 1/4	25	ANR pf	2.67	10.3	...	6	26	26	26	...
6	1 7/8	ATT Cap wt	...	...	...	20	5 7/8	5 3/4	5 3/4	- 1/4
s 22 3/4	14	AVEMCO	.40	1.9	17	6	21 1/2	21 3/8	21 1/2	...
84 1/4	40	BrlNth	2.20	3.7	13	2701	59 3/8	58 1/4	58 3/4	+ 1/2
4 3/4	1/2	Brooke rt	...	...	...	26	4 5/8	4 5/8	4 5/8	...
7	2 1/2	CV REIT	.25	4.0	...	10	6 3/8	6 1/4	6 1/4	...
3 1/8	2 1/4	CalifREIT	.40	13.9	...	3	2 7/8	2 7/8	2 7/8	...
39 3/8	17 7/8	Circus wi	...	...	...	14	39 1/4	38 7/8	39 1/4	+ 5/8
82 1/2	39 5/8	Dsny	.32	.6	17	6211	53 3/4	52	53 1/4	+1 1/4
38 3/8	19 1/2	Fubar	.24	.9	13	z 1454	28	26 7/8	27 3/8	+ 1/4
8 3/4	3 5/8	Navistr	...	...	...	6484	4 1/2	4 1/8	4 1/4	...

EXPLANATORY NOTES
The following explanations apply to New York and American Exchange listed issues and the National Association of Securities Dealers Automated Quotations system's over-the-counter securities.
The 52-week high and low columns show the highest and lowest price of the issue during the preceding 52 weeks. Dividend rates, unless noted, are annual disbursements. Yield is the dividends paid by a company on its securities, expressed as a percentage of price. The PE ratio is determined by dividing the price of a share of stock by its company's earnings. Sales figures are quoted in 100s (00 omitted). a-Extra dividend. b-Annual rate of the cash dividend and a stock dividend was paid. n-Newly issued in the past 52 weeks. pf-Preferred. rt-Rights. s-Stock split or dividend greater than 25% in the past 52 weeks. vi-In bankruptcy or receivership. wd-When distributed. wi-When issued. wt-Warrants. ww-With warrants. x-Ex-dividend or ex-rights. xw-Without warrants. z-Sales in full, not in hundreds.

investment, even though as a shareholder he is an owner of the business. If the management of the company loses money and the company goes bankrupt, the debts of the company could not be assessed against the investors. Their risk would be limited to the amount of money they had in the company's stock.

Equity investments have risks as well as rewards. These risks include the potential for market losses if the price of the stock decreases, loss of capital through failure of the business and decrease in income if dividends are cut.

Preferred Stock

In addition to common stock, a corporation will often issue a second type of stock called *preferred stock*. Although preferred stockholders also acquire equity in the corporation, they usually do not have the same voting rights as the holders of common stock. As the term "preferred" indicates, however, they do enjoy some privileges not granted common stockholders—primarily in that they enjoy a preference over the holders of common stock in the receipt of dividends.

To many people, preferred stock appears to be a cross between an equity and a debt security. Although it is an equity security and represents ownership in the issuing corporation, it does not provide all of the privileges of ownership that are normally associated with common stock. Unlike common stock, most preferred stock is issued as nonvoting stock. Preferred stocks usually do not carry either voting rights or **preemptive rights** (that is, the right to buy additional shares in a new offering before those shares are offered to the general public).

Like a debt instrument, preferred stock is often (though not always) issued as a fixed income security with a stated dividend. Its price fluctuations tend to be affected more by changes in interest rates than by the outlook for the company. Preferred stock has no preset date at which it matures or is scheduled for redemption by the corporation (unlike corporate bonds or other debt securities).

Although preferred stock typically does not have the same growth potential as common stock (because its price is more likely to be affected by changes in interest rates than by changes in company profits), the owners of preferred stock generally have an advantage over common stockholders in two ways:

- When dividends are declared by the board of directors, owners of cumulative preferred stock receive their dividends (plus any dividends in arrears) first.
- If a corporation goes bankrupt after paying off creditors, preferred stockholders have a prior claim on the remaining assets—common stockholders' claims are typically the last ones paid.

Dividends (once they have been declared by the board of directors) must be paid to preferred stockholders before they can be paid to common stockholders. This gives holders of preferred stock a higher probability of receiving regular income than the holders of common stock. To most owners of preferred stock, the stock's most attractive feature is its fixed dividend (although preferred stocks with variable dividends exist, they are less common).

Preferred stock is issued in a variety of forms, each carrying different types of rights. Following are descriptions of a few of the different kinds of preferred stock issued by companies.

Prior Preferred

Prior preferred stock, as its name indicates, has a priority claim over other preferred stock in receiving dividends, as well as in the distribution of assets in the event of liquidation. Because of this advantage, prior preferred is usually issued with a slightly lower dividend rate than other preferred.

Cumulative Preferred

Owners of cumulative preferred stock have the right to receive any missed dividends before any dividends are paid to the owners of common stock. If a corporation is experiencing financial difficulties, its board of directors may vote to reduce or suspend payment of dividends to both common and preferred stockholders. Common stockholders do not have any recourse if this occurs; any dividends they miss may (or may not) be made up by the corporation at a later date. When the company is able to resume full payment of dividends, holders of cumulative preferred stock will receive the current preferred dividend plus the total accumulated dividends (dividends in arrears) before any dividends are distributed to common stockholders.

Participating Preferred

In addition to the fixed dividend characteristic of other classes of preferred stock, participating preferred stock offers its owners another benefit. These stockholders receive a share (usually expressed as a percentage of the stock's par value) of any corporate profits that remain after all dividends due other securities are paid.

Convertible Preferred

A preferred stock is convertible if the holder has the right to convert its shares into shares of common stock at some future point in time. Because the value of convertible preferred is linked to the value of common stock in this way, it tends to fluctuate more in price than do other fixed income securities.

Convertible preferred is usually issued with a lower stated dividend rate than nonconvertible preferred, due to the special advantages it offers stockholders.

Callable Preferred

Often, a corporation may decide to issue a special class of stock known as *callable (redeemable) preferred*. With this type of stock, a company retains the right to call (or buy back) the stock from investors. Companies often issue preferred stock with a call feature during periods of high interest rates. The right to call back the stock allows them to eliminate a relatively high fixed dividend obligation sometime in the future and sell in its stead an issue of preferred stock with a lower dividend.

□ DEBT SECURITIES

Bonds of various types (including those issued by municipalities, corporations, the U.S. government and governmental agencies) are commonly referred to as *debt securities*; that is, they represent a loan by an investor to the issuer. In return for this loan, the issuer promises both to repay the principal of the debt at a specified date in the future and to pay the investor interest on the amount borrowed. Because the interest rate an investor receives is normally set by the issuer at the time the bond is issued, bonds are also referred to as *fixed income securities.*

A bond represents an issuer's promise to repay money it has borrowed (the principal of the loan) at some point in the future. The individual bonds that make up the entire bond issue usually have a face (or par) value of $1,000 each.

The maturity date (the date on which the loan principal is to be repaid to the investor) varies from bond to bond and from issuer to issuer. Investors can find bonds with maturities ranging from a few months to many years in today's market.

Unlike stockholders, bondholders do not have ownership interest in the issuing corporation (or government body) or a voting right. In return for their investment, bondholders receive the issuer's promise to repay principal and pay interest on the debt. As creditors of the issuer, corporate bondholders receive preferential treatment over common and preferred stockholders in most instances. When a corporation files for bankruptcy, the claims of creditors (including bondholders) are settled before the claims of stockholders. For this reason, bonds are sometimes called *senior securities.*

Most investors buy bonds for a secure source of income and safety of principal. While bonds offer these benefits, there are risks associated with owning any debt security. One risk is inflation risk (also known as *purchasing power risk*). As the value of money falls over time, the purchasing power of a debt security and its interest payments falls too. The $1,000 invested in 1980 cannot buy as much today as it could then. Therefore, in a period of high inflation, it is possible for a bond investor to end up with less purchasing power than when he started, even after earning interest.

A second risk is interest rate risk. If interest rates rise, the price at which a bond can be sold will generally decline. For example, an investor pays $1,000 for a bond with an 8% interest rate; a year later, the investor decides to sell the bond, but finds that interest rates on comparable bonds have risen to 9%. No one will now pay the investor $1,000 for an 8% bond if a similar bond paying 9% can be bought for $1,000. Therefore, to offset the interest rate difference, the investor will likely have to settle for less than $1,000. Of course, if the investor is prepared to wait until the bond matures, the issuer is still obligated to repay the $1,000. Interest rate risk can, however, also work in the investor's favor. If interest rates decline, bond prices generally rise.

A third risk is credit risk. The market value of a bond will decline if question arises about the ability of the issuer either to make interest payments on the bond or to redeem the bond at maturity.

Issuers of Debt Securities

Corporations. Debt issued by corporations (also known as *funded debt*) includes both short-term debt (notes) and long-term debt (bonds). Long-term debt securities are an important source of corporate capital for plant construction, equipment purchases and working capital.

U.S. government and government agencies. The federal government is not only the nation's largest borrower, it is also its most secure credit risk. The bills, notes and bonds it issues to finance operations are backed by the full faith and credit of the government and by the government's almost unlimited powers of taxation.

Municipalities. Municipal securities are the debt obligations of state and local governments and their agencies. Most are issued to raise capital to finance public works and construction projects that benefit the general public (as opposed to financing the municipality's current expenses).

Corporate Bonds

There are two types of corporate bonds: secured debt (secured by a specific pledge of assets), and debentures (secured only by the corporation's promise to pay).

Secured bonds are issued by corporations and may be backed by real estate, equipment, stock and other assets. In recent years, some bonds issued by finance companies have been secured by accounts receivable and notes on auto loans and consumer credit balances. Mortgage bonds are bonds that are secured with the pledge of a specific piece of real estate. In the event of a default, the trustee has the right to claim the property on behalf of the bondholders. Any additional value after bondholder claims have been met goes to meeting the other obligations of the company.

FIGURE 3   Example of Corporate Bond Quotes

New York Exchange Corporate Bonds
Quotations as of 4 pm Eastern Time
Friday, July 16, 1995

Volume $45,198,000

Bonds	Cur Yld	Vol	High	Low	Close	Net Chg.
AForP 5s 30r	9.6	50	52 1/4	51 7/8	52	+3/4
AbbtL 7 5/8s 96	7.6	21	99 3/4	99 3/4	99 3/4	...
Advst 9s 08	cv	72	103 1/2	103	103	...
AetnLf 8 1/8s 07	8.5	15	95 3/4	95 3/4	95 3/4	- 1
AirbF 7 1/2s 11	cv	32	114	112	114	+1
AlaP 9s 2000	8.9	18	100 3/4	100 5/8	100 3/4	+1/4
AlaP 8 1/2s 01	8.6	13	98 3/8	98 3/8	98 3/8	- 3/8
AlaP 8 7/8s 03	9.5	65	102 7/8	102 1/2	102 1/2	- 3/8
AlldC zr 92	...	10	91 1/2	91 1/8	91 1/2	- 1/8
viAmes 7 1/2s 14f	cv	79	15 1/2	14 3/4	15	+1
Ancp 13 7/8s 02f	cv	10	91	89 3/8	91	+2

EXPLANATORY NOTES

Yield is current yield. cv-Convertible bond. dc-Deep discount. f-Dealt in flat. m-Matured bonds, negotiability impaired by maturity. na-No accrual. r-Registered. zr-Zero coupon. vi-In bankruptcy or receivership or being reorganized.

Debentures have no specific collateral backing. Rather, they are backed by the good faith and general credit of the issuer. The owner of a debenture is considered a general creditor of the company.

Figure 3 shows an example of corporate bond quotations as they might appear in the business section of a newspaper.

U.S. Government and Agency Bonds

U.S. Government Debt

Securities issued by the U.S. government (or by governmental agencies) are backed by its "full faith and credit." This backing is largely based on its power to raise money through taxation.

The Public Debt Act of 1942 gave the U.S. Treasury department the authority to determine the number and types of government securities to be sold to meet the needs of the federal budget. The Treasury, however, does not set the interest rate on its new issues; the marketplace does. (Buyers indicate the interest rates they are willing to accept by withholding their bids if the rates proposed are too low.) The marketplace also dictates, to a degree, the form and features of those securities. In general, U.S. government securities are exempt from state and municipal taxation, but are subject to federal taxation.

Some government securities are issued in definitive form, which means that the investor receives a certificate. Others are issued in book-entry form; that is, the investor's name is stored in a computer, and the investor receives no certificate.

Treasury bonds are the long-term obligations of the U.S. government. These bonds are issued with terms ranging from 10 to 30 years. They are issued with fixed interest rates and term maturities. Interest is payable every six months and is not taxable for state and local purposes.

Treasury notes are the medium-term debt issued by the government with maturities from one year to ten years, although the typical minimum maturity at issue is two years. T notes are interest-bearing securities with interest payment every six months. They are issued in multiples of $1,000 with a minimum purchase of $5,000 for bonds maturing in less than five years.

Treasury bills are the shortest term debt securities offered by the U.S. government. T bills differ from bonds and notes in that they do not pay a stated rate of interest. Instead, T bills are sold at a discount from their face value and redeemed by the government at face value. The difference between the issue price and the face (par) value is the interest earned by an investor in a T bill. A quote of 5.50% discount rate or discount yield, for example, means that a one-year T bill is selling at 5 1/2% less than its face value. For a $10,000 52-week Treasury bill, that would be a price of $9,450. However, an investor's yield to maturity is somewhat higher than the stated discount yield because the investor's outlay is less than the full $10,000.

T bills are offered weekly by the U.S. Treasury with maturities of 13, 26 and even, sometimes, 52 weeks. At maturity, the investor can either request cash or request that the amount be rolled over into another T bill. They are sold in minimum amounts of $10,000 and multiples of $5,000 thereafter.

Government Agency Debt

Congress authorizes certain agencies of the federal government to issue marketable debt securities. Some of these agencies for which transactions are reported daily in many newspapers are:

- Federal Farm Credit Banks
- Federal Home Loan Mortgage Corporation (FHLMC or Freddie Mac)
- Government National Mortgage Association (GNMA or Ginnie Mae)

Other agency-like organizations that are operated by private corporations include:

- Federal Home Loan Banks (FHLBs)
- Federal National Mortgage Association (FNMA or Fannie Mae)

The term "agency" is sometimes used to refer to entities that are not technically government agencies, but that do have ties to the government. The Federal Home Loan Banks, for example, are owned by the private savings and loan associations that are members of the FHLB system. Yet the FHLB operates under federal charter and regulates its members. Whatever its technical status, therefore, it functions as a government agency. The Federal National Mortgage Association (Fannie Mae) also is privately owned but government regulated.

Agency issues sell at higher yields than do direct obligations of the federal government (partially attributable to a slightly higher level of risk), but they frequently sell at lower yields than those available on corporate debt securities. The maturities of these issues vary from very short term to relatively long term.

Agency issues have a very slight risk of failing to pay interest and principal because the issuing agency backs them with revenues from taxes, fees or income from lending activities. Agency issues are backed in several ways: by collateral, such as cash, U.S. Treasury securities and the debt obligations; by a U.S. Treasury guarantee; by the right of the agency to borrow from the Treasury; or, in a few cases, by the full faith and credit of the government.

Municipal Debt

Municipal securities represent loans by investors to a state, political subdivision of a state or U.S. territory. They are issued by municipalities (like corporations issue other debt obligations) to raise capital. Most of the capital raised through a municipal bond issue is used to finance public works and construction projects (capital improvements) that benefit the general public. Examples of these projects and improvements include construction and maintenance of streets and highways, water distribution and sewage systems, and public welfare and health services. The wide range of maturities available in municipal issues (from one month to 50 years or more) is an attractive feature to investors because the flexibility this offers allows an investor to tailor a portfolio of municipal securities to fit specific investment needs and financial plans.

In the ranking of investments by safety of principal, U.S. government and U.S. government agency securities are considered the safest. The degree of safety of municipal bonds varies from issue to issue and from municipality to municipality. Much of the safety of any municipal issue is based on the viability of the issuing municipality and the community in general.

The interest paid by most municipal securities is exempt from federal income taxation. The federal government does not tax the interest received from debt obligations of municipalities; municipalities reciprocate by not taxing the interest from federal debt securities. This **doctrine of reciprocal immunity** was established by the U.S. Supreme Court. To qualify for the exemption from federal taxation, the municipal security must be issued to fund government (public rather than private) activities.

There are only two major categories of municipal security issues: **general obligation bonds** (GOs—bonds backed by the full faith, credit and taxing powers of the municipal borrower) and **revenue bonds** (bonds backed by revenues generated by the financed facility).

GO bondholders have a legal claim to the revenues received by a municipal government for payment of the principal and interest due them. GOs are used to raise funds for those municipal capital improvements that typically do not produce revenues (building a new city hall, for example). Their financial support is ad valorem taxes (which means *according to the value of* the property) for city, county and district bonds and sales and income taxes for state bonds. GOs are also known as *full faith and credit bonds*.

Revenue bonds are payable only from the earnings of specific revenue-producing enterprises. An analysis of the quality of revenue bonds would include sources of revenue, feasibility studies, maturity structure, call provisions, application of revenues and protective covenants of the indenture. Unlike GOs, revenue bonds are subject to no statutory debt limits and require no voter approval. Revenue bonds may be issued by any municipally authorized political entity.

Rating and Analyzing Bonds

Various **rating** services, such as Standard & Poor's, Moody's and Fitch, evaluate and publish their ratings of bond issues. Standard & Poor's and Moody's rate both corporate and municipal bonds; Fitch rates corporate bonds, municipal bonds and commercial paper. All three base their bond ratings primarily on the issuer's creditworthiness—that is, on the projected ability of the issuer to make interest and principal payments as they come due. The less likely the issuer is able to make payments as promised, the lower the rating given the bond. If the prospects are good that the issuer will be able to make the required payments and make them on time, the bond will be granted a high rating.

The ratings on bonds may change over time. If the issuer's ability to make interest and principal payments changes after the bond is first issued, the rating services will reevaluate the bond and change their ratings as necessary.

Figure 4 shows bond ratings as they are used by Standard & Poor's and Moody's rating services.

Investment grade. The Comptroller of the Currency, the Federal Deposit Insurance Corporation (FDIC), the Federal Reserve and state banking authorities have established policies determining which securities banks can purchase. A municipal bond must be considered of investment grade (that is, with a Standard & Poor's rating of BBB or higher or a Moody's rating of Baa or higher) to be suitable for purchase by banks. Investment grade bonds are the same as bank grade bonds. Bonds rated BBB or Baa may involve some uncertainty, but banks may still buy them.

Finer gradations of these categories are also possible. A plus or minus sign in a Standard & Poor's rating indicates that the bond rates near the

FIGURE 4   Examples of Bond Rating Systems

Standard & Poor's	Moody's	Interpretation
Bank grade (investment grade) bonds		
AAA	Aaa	Highest rating. Capacity to repay principal and interest judged high.
AA	Aa	Very strong. Only slightly less secure than the highest rating.
A	A	Judged to be slightly more susceptible to adverse economic conditions.
BBB	Baa	Adequate capacity to repay principal and interest. Slightly speculative.
Speculative (non-investment grade) bonds		
BB	Ba	Speculative. Significant chance that issuer could miss an interest payment.
B	B	Issuer has missed one or more interest or principal payments.
C	Caa	No interest is being paid on bond at this time.
D	D	Issuer is in default. Payment of interest or principal is in arrears.

top or bottom of that particular category; thus, an A– bond is of poorer quality than an A+ bond. Moody's uses numbers to indicate position within a category; thus, an A1 bond is of higher quality than an A3 bond. Moody's also provides ratings for short-term municipal notes, designating MIG 1 as the highest quality and MIG 4 as the lowest.

Specific criteria used to rate corporate and municipal bonds include:

- the amount and composition of existing debt;
- the stability of the issuer's cash flow;
- the ability of the issuer to meet scheduled payments of interest and principal on its debt obligations;
- asset protection; and
- management ability.

Relationship of Rating to Yield

Generally, the higher the bond rating, the lower the yield. Investors are willing to accept a lower return on their investments if they expect their principal to be safe and their annual interest payments to be more predictable.

Zero-coupon Bonds

A relatively recent addition to the bond market, zero-coupon bonds do not have interest coupons attached, nor do the issuers make annual interest payments. Investors who purchase them, therefore, do not receive periodic interest. Instead, they purchase a bond at a price lower than the bond's $1,000 par value and can redeem it for par on the maturity date. The "interest" earned on the bond is the difference between the price paid initially and the amount received at maturity. Zero-coupon bonds are issued both by corporations and by municipalities, and they may be created by broker-dealers from other types of securities, including those issued by the federal government.

Brokerage firms have the permission of the Treasury department to create zero-coupon bonds (Treasury receipts) from U.S. Treasury notes and bonds. Broker-dealers buy Treasury securities, then sell the principal and coupons separately to investors, pricing them at a discount from face value. You can think of a $1,000 Treasury note with a 6% coupon as a number of separate obligations: the obligation to pay $30 in six months, in a year, in a year and a half, and so on to maturity and the obligation to pay $1,000 at maturity. The broker that buys the note can resell each of those obligations separately.

Money-market Securities

In the financial marketplace, a distinction is made between the **capital market** and the **money market**. The capital market serves as a source of intermediate- to long-term funding for corporations and municipal and federal governments. This funding usually takes the form of debt and equity securities with maturities of more than one year.

The money market, on the other hand, exists to provide very short-term funds to corporations, municipalities and the U.S. government. The money-market securities that generate these funds are primarily short-term debt issues and loans.

The U.S. economy requires a constant availability of short-term funds, both cash and credit. Banks must be able to meet demands for cash immediately, even if those demands are unusually large. Businesses must be able to finance current operations as bills come due. Municipalities must pay salaries, services and contractors while waiting for revenues or bond issues to generate money. Money-market instruments provide ways for businesses, financial institutions and governments to meet their short-term obligations and cash requirements.

The business of the money market is to shift funds from institutions with temporary excesses of money to institutions with temporary deficiencies. Among the borrowers in the money market are the U.S. Treasury, large commercial banks, corporations, dealers in money-market instruments and many states and municipalities. Large institutions such as banks, trust companies and insurance companies are often lenders and buyers of money-market instruments.

Because they are short-term instruments, money-market securities offer investors a highly liquid investment. Money-market instruments also provide investors with a relatively high degree of safety; most issuers of money-market securities have high credit ratings.

Money-market securities are issued by a number of different entities. Money-market instruments issued by the U.S. government and its agencies include:

- Treasury bills;
- Federal Farm Credit Bank short-term notes and bonds maturing in one year;
- Federal Home Loan Bank (FHLB) short-term discount notes and interest-bearing notes;
- Federal National Mortgage Association (FNMA) short-term discount notes; and
- short-term discount notes issued by various smaller agencies.

Municipalities issue tax-exempt money-market instruments that include:

- bond anticipation notes (BANs)
- tax anticipation notes (TANs)
- revenue anticipation notes (RANs)
- construction loan notes (CLNs)
- tax and revenue anticipation notes (TRANs)

Corporations and banks have a number of methods for raising short-term funds in the money market, including:

- repurchase agreements (repos)
- reverse repurchase agreements
- bankers' acceptances (time drafts)
- commercial paper (prime paper)
- negotiable certificates of deposit
- federal funds
- brokers' and dealers' loans

□ SPECIAL SECURITIES

Not all securities fit neatly into the categories of equity and debt. Corporations with special financing or cash flow timing needs may not be able to meet these needs by issuing stocks or bonds. For this reason, a number of special securities have evolved to fill the gaps.

Convertible Bonds

Some corporate securities may be converted by their owner into other securities of the same corporation (such as bonds into stock). These securities are called *convertibles* and are usually debentures, subordinated debentures or preferred stock.

Technically, convertible bonds are classified as debt securities. Their holders are creditors of the corporation. But convertible debentures, in reality, are like both debt and equity securities. Though they have a fixed interest rate and a maturity date established at the time of issuance, they can also be converted into common stock of the issuing corporation.

A corporation might add a conversion feature to its bonds and preferred stock issues so as to make them more marketable. For example, during periods when investors are interested in stocks and the market for new fixed income securities is poor, the conversion privilege makes a bond more attractive. In exchange for the investor benefits offered by a conversion feature, many corporations will pay a lower rate of interest on convertible securities.

When the bond market is strong, convertible debentures are frequently issued as a means of raising equity capital on a postponed basis. When (and if) the debentures are converted, the corporation's capitalization changes from debt to equity.

Theoretically, the convertible bondholder has the best of two markets: the investment safety of the fixed income market and the potential appreciation of the equity market. Critics of convertible securities contend that convertibles do not necessarily offer the best of the equity and debt markets. The critics say that convertibles do not offer interest rates commensurate with lack of principal safety (nonconvertible debentures offer higher interest yields) and have a tendency to depress common stock prices because of the possible dilution effect.

Stock Rights

When issuing new shares of common stock, a corporation may choose to sell its shares to existing stockholders before going to public investors. This may be because the company believes its stockholders would be the best prospects to buy additional shares of the company, or it may be because the corporation's stockholders have preemptive rights.

The term "preemptive right" refers to the right of an existing stockholder to purchase shares of a new issue of stock in proportion to the number of shares the investor already owns. A concern is that if new shares are issued by a corporation, the present stockholders' ownership of the company will be diluted if they are not able to purchase a proportionate share of the new issue; their voting percentage, earnings per share and net worth per share will be reduced. Furthermore, the additional supply of stock available to the market may cause the market price of the stock to decrease.

The stock rights entitle the stockholder to purchase common stock below the current market price at issue date. This means that the rights are valued separately and trade in the secondary market during the subscription period.

A rights offering is a short-term (typically 30 to 45 days) privilege a stockholder receives from a corporation, and a subscription right is the actual certificate representing that privilege. One right is issued for each share of common stock the investor owns. Therefore, an investor with 100 shares of common stock receives a certificate representing 100 rights.

The terms of the offering are stipulated in the subscription rights, which are mailed to stockholders on the payable date. The rights describe the new shares to which the stockholder is entitled to subscribe, the price, the date the new stock will be issued, the name of the rights agent that will send the subscription and the final date for exercising those rights.

Stock Warrants

A stock warrant is a certificate giving the holder the right to purchase securities at a stipulated price from the issuer. Unlike a right, a warrant is usually a long-term instrument, affording the investor the option of buying shares at a later date at the subscription price, subject to the warrant's expiration date.

Warrants may be detachable from the underlying security, or they may be nondetachable. If detachable, they may trade separately in the market purely as speculation on the price of the underlying stock (because the warrants do not receive dividends or represent any other right of a corporate owner). While the exercise price is set above the market price of the stock when the warrant is first issued, the investor hopes the stock's price will increase, at which point the investor can (1) exercise the warrant and buy the stock below the price he would have to pay in the market or (2) sell the warrant in the market at a price based on the benefit the purchaser can get by exercising the warrant and buying the stock below market price.

Warrants are usually offered to the public as a sweetener in connection with other securities (usually debentures) to make these securities more attractive to investors. Investors enjoy the security of owning a bond, note or preferred stock, but might also benefit from the opportunity to participate in the appreciation of the common stock.

FIGURE 5   Convertible Debt and ADRs as Quoted by NASDAQ

NASDAQ Bid & Asked Quotations

Quotations as of 4 pm Eastern Time
Tuesday, September 13, 1998

Convertible Debentures

ADRs

Debenture	Sales 100s	Bid	Asked	Net Chg.	Stock & Div	Sales 100s	Bid	Asked	Net Chg.
AirWtr 8s 15	...	84	87	...	AngSA 1.15	23	37 1/4	37 7/8	+ 5/8
AmWst 7s11	50	15 1/2	20	...	AngAG .42	65	7 3/8	7 5/8	...
Brunos 09	800	131 1/2	134	...	ASEA 2.08	111	59 1/4	59 3/4	+1 1/4
Chirn 7 1/4 15	140	129	131	+1	Blyvor .13	23	2 1/4	2 7/16	...
Hechng cv 12	...	66	68	+1	Bwater .50	5	9 3/4	10 1/8	...
MCI Cm 04	950	38 1/2	39 1/4	...	Buffels 1.65	38	13 1/8	13 1/2	...
Masco 11	...	55 1/2	57 1/2	...	BurmC .37	5	17 1/4	17 5/8	- 1/8

American Depositary Receipts

Americans buying stock of foreign corporations need not always arrange to receive the foreign certificates. Instead, the investor can, in many cases, buy American depositary receipts (ADRs). ADRs facilitate the transfer of U.S. investments in foreign corporations, and the ADR itself is an instrument that can, like a stock, be bought and sold in the U.S. securities markets on an exchange or over the counter.

An ADR is a negotiable receipt for a given number of shares of stock (typically one to ten) in a non-U.S. corporation. The foreign stock certificate that the ADR represents remains in the custody of a foreign bank, and the ADRs themselves are issued by foreign branches of large commercial U.S. banks. The stock must remain on deposit as long as the ADR is outstanding because the ADR is the depository bank's guarantee that it holds the stock.

Figure 5 contains examples of convertible debt and ADR quotations.

□ SUMMARY

This chapter covered the three basic categories of investments: equity, debt and special securities. Common and preferred stock provide a means for investors to share in the ownership of a corporation, and a means for corporations to raise money by dividing their ownership among willing investors. Bonds and debentures represent loans from investors with excess cash to companies that are willing to pay interest for the privilege of using that cash for a period of time. Special securities, such as convertible bonds, stock rights and warrants and ADRs, give companies additional flexibility in meeting their financing needs.

In the next chapter, we will take a look at two other categories of investments—packaged products (such as mutual funds and direct participation programs) and derivative products (such as options and commodities futures). We will discuss the events that led to the creation of each and how they are used by today's investors and the securities industry.

☐ REVIEW

Check how well you have learned the information contained in this chapter by completing the following sentences.

An ownership interest in a corporation is known as

_____

(See page 13)

An advantage of equity investments is that they offer limited

_____

(See page 15)

Preferred stock has been given a preference over common in the receipt of

_____

(See page 16)

The three primary issuers of debt securities are

_____

(See page 18)

The federal government does not tax the interest from municipal securities, and municipalities do not tax the interest of federal securities under the doctrine of

_____

(See page 24)

A municipal security that is rated BBB/Baa or higher is considered

_____

(See page 25)

Businesses, financial institutions and governments can meet their needs for short-term cash through

_____

(See page 28)

The right of an existing shareholder to purchase shares of a new issue is known as

_____

(See page 30)

Chapter 3

Packaged and Derivative Products

"Securities markets can provide a vital ingredient in economic growth by pooling the funds of investors across an entire country."
Richard C. Breeden, SEC Chairman

Overview

As the needs of corporations and investors became more complex, simple equity and debt securities were no longer able to meet the full range of these needs. The securities industry responded with innovative solutions. Some investment firms began to package some types of securities together, in the process altering the characteristics of the underlying investments enough to create new products, such as mutual funds and direct participation programs. Other investment firms and exchanges created entirely new products, such as options and commodities futures. These newer products allow individuals and financial institutions to tailor the risk profiles of their investment portfolios to more closely fit their needs.

This chapter describes the features and benefits of and markets for these packaged and derivative products.

□ PACKAGED PRODUCTS

Portfolio diversification is an important means by which investors can lower their investment risks. By spreading investable funds over a number of securities, investors will experience less of a loss if a single security does not perform as well as expected. Individual investors cannot always afford the money or time to adequately diversify their portfolios, however, because it would involve buying, selling and managing a large number of individual securities. In answer to this problem, the securities industry has developed a wide range of packaged products that provide investors with all of the benefits of diversification for a relatively low initial investment.

The packaged products currently offered include investment company securities (mutual funds), unit investment trusts, real estate investment trusts and direct participation programs.

Investment Companies

Investment companies are corporations or trusts that purchase securities with investors' pooled resources. The investors receive shares or units in the investment companies' portfolios. Investment gains and losses, dividends and interest income, and the expenses of managing the assets are distributed to the investors proportionately.

Management Companies

The majority of investment companies are classified as *management companies*. At the end of 1991, the total number of mutual funds had exceeded 3,431, and total industry assets were $1.3 trillion.

Managed investment companies actively buy, sell and trade securities, which are held in the companies' portfolios according to a specific investment objective (as stated in the companies' prospectus).

Closed-end companies. A closed-end company issues a fixed number of shares in its investment portfolio. After the initial public offering, its shares are publicly traded in the secondary markets (on an exchange or OTC), where supply and demand determine the price of each share in the portfolio.

Closed-end management companies may issue more than one class of security (including preferred stock and bonds), but are not permitted to borrow from a bank.

Open-end companies (mutual funds). An open-end management company continuously issues new fund shares to investors who wish to buy, and redeems fund shares from investors who wish to sell. Due in part to this continuous process of issuing and redeeming shares, the capitalization of an open-end company is constantly changing. Upon request of a shareholder, open-end companies must redeem his shares at net asset value (NAV). The NAV of individual fund shares is determined by the fund's portfolio value (the value of its investments) divided by the number of shares outstanding.

Characteristics of Mutual Funds

Advantages to investors. Mutual funds (open-end investment companies) offer investors several advantages. Of primary importance to investors is a mutual fund's guaranteed liquidity; that is, investors can readily "cash out" their mutual fund shares. An open-end mutual fund must redeem shares presented to it by investors at the NAV within seven days (although the company may require a written request for redemption).

A second advantage offered to investors in mutual funds is professional portfolio management. Investment decisions for the funds are made by full-time professional advisers—a luxury few investors can afford when investing independently.

Mutual fund shares also offer diversification. Mutual funds provide a greater degree of diversification than most private investors are able to achieve independently.

Finally, many mutual funds offer investors a variety of convenience features. These may include check-writing privileges against fund balances, automatic reinvestment of dividends, monthly payment of dividends, and the ability to exchange shares from one mutual fund to another in the "family" of funds offered by an investment company.

Investment objectives. Funds are available to meet the investment objectives of most investors, and a mutual fund prospectus identifies the fund's objectives. Although the most common fund objectives include growth and income, the variety of mutual funds available today means that almost any investment objective can be met by an investment in mutual funds. Following are some examples of mutual fund objectives.

- **Growth funds.** Growth funds invest in the equity securities of those companies that are expected to grow more rapidly than the typical company. Growth companies tend to retain all or most of their earnings for research and development and reinvest profits in the companies rather than pay out dividends. As a result, the appreciation of share value is the primary objective of the funds.
- **Income funds.** Income funds seek to provide current yield. The investments in such funds may consist of debt securities, equity securities or both. The investor who selects income funds is more interested in current income than in potential growth.
- **Balanced funds.** In a balanced fund, different types of securities are purchased according to a preset formula. For example, a balanced fund's portfolio might contain 60% equity securities and 40% debt securities. These percentages could change as the prospects for each asset change. For example, if the stock market turns bullish, the portfolio manager could increase the percentage invested in equities and decrease the percentage invested in debt.
- **Bond and preferred stock funds.** The objective of bond and preferred stock funds is safety of principal and enhanced income.
- **Tax-exempt funds.** Tax-exempt funds contain instruments that produce tax-exempt income. Common types of tax-exempt funds include municipal bond and tax-exempt money-market funds.
- **U.S. government funds.** U.S. government funds purchase securities backed by the U.S. Treasury; investors in these funds seek current income and maximum safety.
- **Specialized funds.** These funds concentrate investments in a particular group of industries or geographic regions. As examples, there are Asian funds that target investment opportunities in Japan and the Pacific basin, health care funds that invest solely in hospitals, care centers and pharmaceutical firms, and precious metals funds that purchase the securities of mining and processing corporations.
- **Dual-purpose funds.** Dual-purpose funds meet two objectives by issuing two different types of shares—income shares and capital gains shares. Investors seeking income purchase the fund's income

shares and receive the interest and dividends earned by the fund's portfolio. Investors interested in capital gains purchase the fund's gains shares and are credited with all of the gains on portfolio holdings. The two types of shares issued by a dual fund are listed separately in the financial pages.

- **Special situation funds.** A special situation fund buys for its portfolio securities of companies that may benefit from a change within the company or in the economy. Takeover candidates and other special situations are common investments.
- **Money-market funds.** Money-market funds invest in safe, high-yield, short-term debt instruments, including Treasury bills, commercial paper, bankers' acceptances, certificates of deposit (CDs) and short-term bonds.

Money-market Funds

Money-market funds are usually no-load (which means there are no sales charges to customers buying shares, nor are there liquidation charges for customers selling shares), open-ended mutual funds. The largest expense to investors is the management fee, which is usually around .5% of the portfolio asset value being managed. The management invests the fund's capital in money-market instruments that have short maturities. Interest rates are not fixed or guaranteed and change as frequently as daily. Interest earned by these funds is computed daily and credited to customers' accounts monthly. Many funds offer check-writing privileges; in general, however, checks must be written for minimum amounts (such as $250 or more).

Mutual Fund Management

Similar in many ways to a typical corporation, a mutual fund has a board of directors, which is elected by those who have purchased shares in the fund. The board's function is to supervise the operation of the mutual fund.

Investment adviser. The investment company that manages the mutual fund contracts with an investment adviser to manage the portfolio. The adviser's fee is usually a percentage of the value of the portfolio. The percentage charged generally varies according to the size of the fund (the bigger the fund, the smaller the percentage) and the type of investment (equity securities typically carry a higher fee percentage than debt securities). In most cases, transaction costs and the adviser's fee are the two biggest expenses incurred by a fund.

The investment adviser's contract must be approved by either a majority of the shareholders or the board of directors.

Custodian. The fund's assets are held by an independent custodian, usually a commercial bank appointed by the directors. In addition to holding fund assets, the custodian performs other functions, such as receiving and disbursing money, distributing dividends, acting as registrar and receiving clients' payments. The custodian is also paid a fee, but it is less than the manager's fee.

Underwriter. The underwriter (often called the *sponsor* or *distributor*) markets fund shares, prepares sales literature and, in return, receives a percentage of the sales charge paid by the client. The underwriter's compensation is part of the sales charge paid by the client either when shares are purchased or as an annual fee.

Marketing Methods

A fund can use any number of methods to market its shares to the public. Some marketing methods used by various firms include:

- **Fund to underwriter to dealer to investor.** The underwriter sells the shares to the securities dealer at net asset value (NAV) plus the underwriter's concession. The dealer then sells the shares to the investor at the full public offering price (POP).
- **Fund to underwriter to investor.** The underwriter acts as dealer and uses its own sales force to sell shares to the public.
- **Fund to investor.** These funds sell directly to the public without the use of a sales force and often without a sales charge. Funds that do not assess a sales charge at the time of purchase are called *no-load funds* because they are sold at the NAV. Such funds assume all sales expenses.
- **Fund to underwriter to plan company to investor.** Organizations that sell contractual plans for the periodic purchase of mutual fund shares are called *plan companies.* Mutual fund shares are

purchased by the plan company and held in trust for the purchaser under the periodic payment plan. Such plans, called *contractual plans,* assess a maximum of 9% in sales charges over the life of the plan.

Unit Investment Trusts

Unit investment trusts (UITs) are investment companies offering investors many of the same features as mutual funds, such as pooling individual investments in a portfolio of securities. They differ from open- and closed-end funds in that they do not actively manage (buy and sell) the securities in the portfolio. In other words, the portfolio is fixed.

A UIT may be fixed or nonfixed. A typical fixed UIT may purchase a portfolio of bonds. When the bonds in the portfolio have matured, the trust is terminated. The nonfixed UIT is often used by investors interested in purchasing units on a contractual basis. The trust may purchase shares of an underlying mutual fund for the nonfixed UIT portfolio.

UITs typically have a large, diversified portfolio. When assets in the portfolio mature, the funds are usually distributed to the UIT holders as opposed to being reinvested. Units in the UIT offer flow-through tax benefits to investors. Thus, like investors in mutual funds, investors in UITs can participate in a large pool of securities while minimizing the risk associated with owning any one specific security.

UITs generally invest in bonds and other debt securities with fixed interest rates and fixed maturities. As a result, UITs are designed to provide a steady, predictable income. The exception to this is the UIT that invests in instruments that have a variable rate of income. In this case, income would vary depending on the rates earned in the trust.

UITs pay interest on a quarterly or monthly basis, but receive income unevenly throughout the year. Thus, the buyer of the fund pays his share of the accrued interest on the fund's entire position and the seller receives the accrued interest on the pro rata share of the fund's position.

As the bonds in the portfolio mature, UIT holders receive a share of the value of the bonds. UITs are normally set up so that a majority of the bonds mature at approximately the same time, giving the UIT a predictable life span.

Real Estate Investment Trusts

A real estate investment trust (REIT) is a company that manages a portfolio of real estate investments in order to earn profits for shareholders. REITs are often traded publicly. REITs allow gains and profits to pass through to investors; however, investors cannot deduct operating or capital losses.

A REIT pools capital in a manner similar to an investment company. REIT portfolios, however, are composed of professionally managed real estate holdings, typically either in direct ownership of income property or in mortgage loans. Shareholders receive dividends from investment income or capital gains distributions. In a REIT, income flows through to the investors but, unlike in a limited partnership, losses do not.

REITs are organized as trusts or corporations where investors buy shares or certificates of beneficial interest either on stock exchanges or in the OTC market. To avoid being taxed as a corporation, the REIT must receive 75% or more of its income from real estate and distribute 95% or more of its taxable income to shareholders.

Direct Participation Programs

Direct participation programs (DPPs), at one time called *tax shelters,* are businesses organized so that they pass all of their income, gains, losses and tax benefits directly to their owners. The businesses themselves pay no tax directly because tax liability is apportioned among the investors. Most DPPs, which are usually structured as limited partnerships, invest in real estate or oil and gas operations.

Investors in limited partnerships typically do not receive quarterly dividends or semiannual interest payments as they would with many other types of investment securities. Instead, investors in limited partnerships may receive a tax deduction based on their share of partnership losses and either a cash distribution or an increase in taxable income (unaccompanied by cash) based on their share of partnership income. It is this direct participation by investors in the consequences of doing business that gives DPPs their name.

Although DPPs are most compatible with the investment needs of wealthy, sophisticated investors, they can be an important part of many people's portfolios.

Limited partnerships might be formed to run any type of business, but they generally invest in only a few areas—usually those in which the tax incentives and economic benefits are greatest. Real estate, oil and gas, and equipment-leasing programs have, in recent years, made up the vast majority of limited partnerships. Limited partnerships have also invested in coal mining, agriculture, timber, breeding and livestock (primarily cattle and racehorses), art objects and cable television, but such programs constitute a small percentage of existing DPPs due to changes in the tax code, greater difficulty of standardizing such programs, higher initial required investment and overall lower interest from investors.

□ DERIVATIVE PRODUCTS

Not all investments originate as issues of corporations for the purpose of raising capital. A particular class of investments exists because of certain special needs of investors. Among these investments are **options** and **futures contracts**. Both are called *derivative products* because their value is based on—that is, derived from—the value of an underlying asset.

Options

Option contracts serve a multitude of purposes. They can provide investors and business people with a means to invest for income or capital gain, to speculate on securities, markets, foreign currencies and other instruments, or even to hedge or protect positions in other investments.

An option is a **contract** between two people. The purchaser (also known as the *holder, buyer* or *owner*) of the contract has paid money for the *right* to buy or the *right* to sell securities. The seller (or writer) of the option contract, on the other hand, has accepted money for taking on an *obligation*. The option seller *must* buy or *must* sell the specified security if asked to do so by the option's buyer. A stock option contract (the kind this text discusses most) represents an agreement between two people (a buyer and seller) to buy or sell 100 shares (a round lot) of stock.

There are two types of options: **calls** and **puts**.

- A call option is the *right to call* (buy) a security from someone for a period of time and at a specific price (the *strike price*). You can buy that right for yourself, or you can sell that right to someone else.
- A put option is the *right to put* (sell) a security to someone for a period of time and at a specific price. You can buy that right for yourself, or you can sell that right to someone else.

A *call* is the right to *buy* a set amount of a specific investment instrument at a set price for a set period of time. A *put* is the right to *sell* a set amount of a specific investment instrument at a set price for a set period of time. The money the buyer of an option contract pays the seller to take on the obligations in the contract is called the option's **premium**.

In theory, options can be created on any item with a fluctuating market value, such as securities, houses, cars, gold coins, baseball cards, playoff tickets and comic books. The most familiar options are those issued on common stocks and called *equity options*.

Options on stock (and some other securities) trade on exchange and OTC markets. Exchange-traded options (also known as *listed options)* have standardized strike prices (that is, the stock price at which the option can be exercised) and bid expiration dates. Options are traded on a number of exchanges, including:

- American Stock Exchange (AMEX)
- Chicago Board Options Exchange (CBOE)
- New York Stock Exchange (NYSE)
- Pacific Stock Exchange (PSE)
- Philadelphia Stock Exchange (PHLX)

In order to qualify for trading on a listed options exchange, the security underlying the option contract must meet minimum listing requirements as specified by that exchange.

Options are traded by brokers on the floors of the option exchanges. These floor brokers buy and sell options the same way they would trade stock—by using hand signals and shouting out their bids or offers on the floor of an exchange in a double-auction market.

The various option exchanges employ market makers and specialists (called *order book officials—OBOs*—on the Pacific and Philadelphia exchanges, OBOs or *board brokers* on the CBOE and *specialists* on the

NYSE and AMEX) to ensure that the auction process runs smoothly. The board brokers and OBOs keep track of limit orders and maintain orderly markets by trading for their own accounts as market makers.

Each market maker on an exchange is responsible for maintaining a fair and orderly market in the options of at least one underlying security. The market maker may hold a position in the option (either long or short) and stands ready to buy or sell the option at any time. The market maker is not required to support a falling market by continuously purchasing the option for his own account.

Broker-dealers often use computerized order routing systems to handle customer option transactions. An order sent through a computerized system will ordinarily be routed from the broker-dealer to the commission-house booth for handling by the exchange member who represents the broker-dealer. The exchange member (the floor broker) will take the order and present it in the trading crowd. If the order is executed, notice of the execution is given back to the commission-house booth, which in turn uses the computerized communication system of the broker-dealer to notify the registered representative and customer.

For some small orders, the routing system may select automatic execution. For quicker action, the system bypasses the commission-house communication booth and floor broker and sends the order directly to the trading post. Each order is executed against an order on the limit order book or a market maker's quote, and the notice of execution is sent directly to the broker-dealer.

The automatic execution system of each exchange has its own criteria, special capabilities and name. The CBOE has the Order Routing System (ORS) and Retail Automatic Execution System (RAES). The AMEX has the Automatic AMEX Options Switch (AUTOAMOS) system. Each offers its subscribers direct communication to and from the trading post.

Options Clearing Corporation

Created and owned by the exchanges that trade options, the Options Clearing Corporation (OCC) is the entity that standardizes option contracts, guarantees performance of the contracts and issues options. The active secondary market in securities options is possible only because of the role of the OCC. The OCC's three-part mission is to standardize options contracts, issue options to buyers and sellers and guarantee performance of the contracts.

On exchange-traded options, the standardized strike prices and expiration months are determined by the OCC. The market itself (that is, interested buyers and sellers) determines the premiums of OCC-issued, standardized options. Options are issued by the OCC without a certificate. The investor's proof of ownership of an option is the trade confirmation and any brokerage account statement received by the customer.

To satisfy the prospectus requirement of the Securities Act of 1933, the OCC publishes an options disclosure document called "The Characteristics and Risks of Standardized Options." This disclosure document outlines the risks and rewards associated with investing in options. An investor must receive this document from the broker-dealer prior to or at the same time as his receiving approval for options trading. The disclosure document must also accompany any options sales literature a client is sent.

Sales literature, according to the options exchanges, does not include material that is strictly educational. A disclosure document does not, for example, have to accompany a letter that explains covered call writing but does not contain specific recommendations. Any educational material, however, must tell the investor where to obtain information on the risks of investing in options.

Index Options

Though options on indexes are relatively new to investors, the indexes themselves are not. Indexes that measure the movements of markets or parts of markets have been around for decades. Two primary types of indexes are important here.

- **Broad-based indexes**. Broad-based indexes are all designed to reflect the movement of the market as a whole, but different indexes vary substantially. Some track as few as 20 stocks; others follow the movements of more than 1,700. Options are available on the S&P 100 Index (ticker symbol OEX), the S&P 500 Index (ticker symbol SPX), the AMEX Major Market Index (ticker symbol XMI) and the *Value Line* Index, among others.
- **Narrow-based indexes**. Narrow-based indexes track the movements of market segments, such as a group of stocks in one

industry or a specific type of investment. Narrow-based indexes include the Technology Index and the Gold/Silver Index.

Indexes provide information; they are not, in themselves, investments. Most investors cannot buy (or sell) an actual index to profit from its changing value. Indexes do provide numerical values that are used to track other investments, however, and these values change. An investor can speculate on the direction, degree and timing of that change by purchasing or selling options on that index. Index options make it possible for investors to profit from the swings in the market or to hedge against losses that market movement can cause in individual stock positions.

Interest Rate Options

Options on government debt securities are a product of the enormous growth of the federal deficit and wide swings in interest rates. Financed by Treasury bills, notes and bonds, the government's deficit creates a vast market in securities that are sensitive to changes in interest rates. Interest rate options were introduced to allow investors to profit from fluctuations in interest rates (and debt security prices) and to hedge the risks created by those fluctuations.

The objectives of investors in interest rate options are similar to those of investors in stock or index options. They hope to profit from changes in the prices of debt securities (caused by fluctuations in interest rates) or to hedge existing portfolios of debt securities against price declines caused by increased interest rates. The securities underlying interest rate options have high values ($100,000 for notes and bonds and $1 million for Treasury bills), and the typical investor tends to be an institution rather than an individual.

Options on debt securities respond to changes in the price of the underlying security just as stock options do. But the values of Treasury bills, notes and bonds move inversely to movements in interest rates. As rates go up, existing debt securities lose value. And as interest rates go down, existing debt securities gain value. A decrease in the interest paid on newly issued bonds will cause the prices of existing bonds that pay higher interest rates to increase. Hence, interest rates have gone down, and debt prices have increased.

Foreign Currency Options

Any U.S. citizen who has traveled outside the United States has learned about currency exchange in the retail market from the sometimes frustrating experience of translating the value of the U.S. dollar into the currency of another country. Currency exchange in the wholesale market of large banks, international corporations and sophisticated investors is similar in complexity and risk.

Investors trade foreign currency options (FCOs) for two reasons: they hope to profit from fluctuating exchange rates, and they want to hedge against the risks arising from fluctuating exchange rates.

Currency risk. The risk in monetary exchange arises from fluctuations in the exchange rate. On a personal scale, this is a fairly simple matter. If a U.S. citizen goes to Canada, for instance, he may be able to exchange each U.S. dollar for $1.30 Canadian. The next time he travels, his U.S. dollar might buy only $1.20 Canadian or it might buy $1.40 Canadian.

U.S. corporations with contracts to buy or sell goods in a foreign country at a specific time have the same problem as the traveler. The dollars a U.S. wholesaler budgets to buy Swiss watches in six months may not be sufficient if the rate of exchange between U.S. dollars and Swiss francs changes in the meantime.

Characteristics of foreign currency options. The Philadelphia Stock Exchange (PHLX) is set up to facilitate the trading of options on foreign currencies. Underlying each FCO is an arbitrary amount of foreign money as set by the exchange. The strike price of the option is set at a certain amount of U.S. money. Each option contract represents the right to buy or sell the foreign currency for the specified amount of U.S. money. The owner of an FCO, therefore, can lock in a certain exchange rate for a certain time, just as the owner of an equity option can lock in the strike price of an equity option.

A call owner can, for the amount of U.S. money set by the strike price, purchase the amount of foreign currency determined by the contract. It is as if the traveler mentioned above could determine months in advance that each of his U.S. dollars would be worth $1.30 Canadian when the time came to travel.

Underlying currencies. Options are available on several foreign currencies, including British pounds, Canadian dollars, German marks, French francs, Japanese yen and Swiss francs. Option contract characteristics vary from currency to currency.

Strategies. Investors and speculators trade FCOs for two reasons: to profit from fluctuating exchange rates or to hedge against the risks arising from fluctuating exchange rates.

Exchange rates rise and fall because of changes in the values of both currencies involved. The changing value of the foreign currency, then, is not the only problem for investors. The value of U.S. money may be changing as well.

The reverse also occurs. Remember that the instrument underlying the option is foreign currency. Whatever is going on with the U.S. dollar, the investor's strategy is determined by the market price of the foreign money. If the dollar is weakening, the deutsche mark could be growing stronger. An investor would be bullish on the mark. To avoid confusion, it helps to concentrate on the underlying instrument, the foreign currency. Remember that the investor has the right to buy or sell the foreign currency, not the U.S. dollar. When an investor expects the value of the underlying instrument to increase, he uses bullish strategies to profit from that increase. That means buying calls or selling puts on the currency. And when an investor expects the value of the currency to drop, he sells calls or buys puts on the currency. Investors can use a variety of other strategies (including *spreads*, which entail buying a call and a put or selling a call and a put) to speculate on the rise and fall of exchange rates.

Hedge strategies. The need to hedge currency exchange is a major reason for the existence of options on currencies. Companies that do business with firms overseas make commitments to spend or receive a given amount of foreign currency weeks or months in the future. Unfortunately, they cannot know precisely what the exchange value of that currency will be. Therefore, when they purchase or sell foreign money on the spot market (the market where commodities are sold for cash and delivered immediately), they may take a beating if its value in U.S. dollars changes. Options on foreign currency provide a way to lessen that risk.

Commodity Futures

A **commodity** is a physical good used in business, in industry and by consumers in everyday life. When you sit down to breakfast in the morning, you are likely to consume a variety of commodities—from bacon to orange juice to the wheat in your toast. Your trip to work depends on even more—the gas and oil in your car, the cotton in your clothes and the coffee you pour when you get there. The route these goods must take on the way into your life is a highly complex one, and sophisticated systems have been put in place over the years to make their delivery as efficient as possible.

The **cash market** for commodities is the marketplace with which people are most familiar. When you buy a frozen pizza at the supermarket, you are engaging in a transaction in the cash market—an immediate exchange of an agreed upon amount of money for an agreed upon quantity of some product. A government bond trader selling 30-year U.S. Treasury bonds to a bank is engaging in a transaction in the cash market. Cash markets can be of any size, range from local to global, and are intended to facilitate the trading of the particular commodity on which they are based.

Negotiated trading. A **cash trade** is a transaction involving the almost immediate exchange of ownership of a commodity or good for an agreed upon amount of money. Cash trading usually takes the form of an agreement privately negotiated between a buyer and a seller to deliver a specified quantity of a good at a time and delivery point on which the parties involved in the transaction have agreed.

The price for the commodity may be established when the transaction is initiated, or it may not be determined until delivery time, at which point it will be based on the then current cash (spot market) value of the commodity.

Participants. Commodity cash markets consist of all of the individuals, corporations and business people involved in the production, warehousing, distribution, processing, manufacture and consumption of basic commodities (food stocks and animal feeds, ore, fossil fuels, livestock and so on). It is these basic goods and resources that are the essential raw materials and base products on which the world's economy is built and on which the quality of human life depends.

The creation and evolution of the various commodity cash markets came about in direct response to the need of business and commerce to channel the flow of goods throughout the economy as efficiently as possible.

Producers of the various commodities, whether the multitude of domestic and foreign grain farmers or the handful of copper mining corporations that control the supply side of that world market, constantly seek the best (highest) price for what they produce. Producers attempt to get the highest possible price for their products (occasionally withholding goods from the market, refusing to harvest crops, or even plowing crops under to artificially lower the supply and thereby support prices). Buyers attempt to purchase raw goods at the lowest possible price to meet their inventory needs. As automobile sales decline, purchasing agents for electrical wire/motor builders may seek out copper substitutes, thus driving the price of copper downward, which in turn may cause commercial copper mining operations to cut back or even to shut down.

Meanwhile, as sellers and buyers continue to negotiate (each hoping to get his optimum price), the middlemen (such as grain elevators and merchants, importers and exporters, pipeline companies and others involved in distribution) attempt to buy at low prices from producers and sell at higher prices to users within the shortest possible time. Most middlemen operate by filling the user's order first (selling), and then buying from a producer as quickly and as cheaply as possible in order to cover the sale and protect the profit margin on the transaction.

Through such bargaining, the cycle of deal making continues daily across the country and around the world. The marketplace consists of cattle auction grounds and stockyards, grain elevators and corporate offices. In fact, face-to-face negotiations account for only a small percentage of all commodity cash market transactions; the bulk of the business is conducted over the phone or by computer.

Although some cash markets are global in nature, most operate locally. For instance, while foreign currencies and government securities markets serve participants around the world and encompass multi-billion dollar trading volumes, cattle markets are typically local businesses that service a limited number of ready buyers and sellers. Because there are fewer participants, these smaller, local markets offer less liquidity and are much more heavily influenced by local supply and demand.

Forward Contracts

Since the invention of money thousands of years ago, the cash trading system has been the primary means of exchanging money for goods. However, trading cash for needed commodities is not always the most efficient method of transacting business. This inefficiency is due in part to the financial burden of delivering the entire dollar amount immediately upon receipt of the goods (settlement), and in part to the expenses associated with the transportation and storage of the often bulky goods until they are needed.

Supply and demand. In addition, there are the problems of supply and demand, both of which can be volatile and unpredictable when cash markets are the only means of trading commodities. For example, when there is no method of "locking in" a price for a later purchase or sale, producers, traders, consumers and middlemen face a difficult choice: to trade at today's price and risk losses if the price of the good then falls, or to delay a trade and risk losses if the good's price rises. Because cash markets do not offer guaranteed prices, it is often difficult to establish an equilibrium between supply and demand, and this instability tends to aggravate price volatility.

Contractual obligations. It is because of such drawbacks that **forward contracts** evolved. Such contracts constitute a direct commitment between one particular buyer and one particular seller. The person selling forward is obligated to make delivery; the person buying forward is obligated to take delivery. A forward contract is nonstandardized in that any terms and provisions contained in it are defined solely by the contract parties, without third-party intervention. This arrangement offers no price protection (hedge) to either side of the contract, but does ensure a ready market or supply source, as it almost always results in delivery.

Because forward contracts represent direct obligations between a particular buyer and seller, only the party on one side of the contract can release the party on the other side from contractual commitments. In addition, because there is no third party guaranteeing performance, each party to the contract assumes the responsibility and risks of checking the credit and trustworthiness of the other.

Elements of a Forward Contract

The five components of a typical forward contract, or cash commodity transaction, are:

1. quantity of the commodity
2. quality of the commodity
3. time for delivery
4. place for delivery
5. price to be paid at delivery

The price for the commodity is usually set at the time the parties enter into the forward contract. In some cases, the agreed on price will be the cash market price at the date of delivery. Sometimes, an investor entering into a forward contract may be required to make a cash deposit or put up an agreed upon amount of money as a margin deposit.

Commodity Futures Market

Certain problems with cash and forward transactions, such as lack of price protection and protection against other risks, gave rise to commodity futures trading. Futures trading is nothing new. In fact, futures contracts evolved from forward contracts that were in use in Europe as early as the Middle Ages.

Exchange regulated. Today, however, futures trading is regulated by an exchange and includes not only those who need to buy or sell the actual commodity, but also those who only wish to speculate on the rise or fall of the product's price over time.

The commodities futures industry serves two functions: (1) as a price-setting marketplace for business people whose livelihoods depend on how efficiently and economically they are able to buy, sell, serve as middlemen for, handle, manage or commercially store bulk commodities and, (2) as a speculative investment market for risk-oriented retail and institutional customers. Although the cash forward market remains an active market, speculative investments account for more than 50% of commodity futures trading.

Futures trades versus cash trades. A futures trade differs from a cash trade in three major respects: (1) it is not personally negotiated between the buyer and seller originating the trade, (2) the trade is always for a specified grade and amount of a commodity (although the contract specifies a certain grade, another grade may be delivered at a discount or a premium to the agreed upon price) and, (3) the commodity must be delivered from the locations and at the times specified by exchange rules. Actual trading takes place on a designated futures contract exchange, which maintains facilities for continuous trading.

Hedging. By using futures, buyers and sellers can protect against adverse price changes. This price protection comes in the form of transfer of risk and is known as *hedging*.

Risk management. Hedging, or risk transfer (also called *risk management)*, is an economic benefit of commodity futures trading. Cash prices are market-determined factors; consequently, producers, middlemen and users of commodities cannot usually accurately predict buying or selling prices at later cash settlement dates. Holding goods in inventory for later sale is risky (remember, though, that risk is not necessarily bad). If, for instance, after a buyer acquires goods for inventory market prices rise, the buyer can sell that inventory at a gain. If prices fall, however, the buyer who holds the goods in inventory suffers an economic loss—if he had waited to purchase, the goods would have cost him less.

Hedging or transferring the price risk can be accomplished by taking an appropriate futures position on the goods the buyer will someday want in inventory. For example, if a cattle breeder owns cows (he could also be said to be "long" cows), he could hedge by establishing a short position in cattle futures (to "short" something is to sell it). The futures position acts as a temporary substitute for the transaction the breeder must enter into at a later time in the cash market. In this example, if the price of the cash stock declines, he will suffer a loss; however, the loss will be offset by a corresponding gain in the futures market.

The futures hedger is transferring price risk to the futures speculator. The speculator takes on the risk of changing prices, while the hedger has taken on the risks only of foregone profit. Those individuals trading futures as speculators will try to gather as much information as possible on which to base trading decisions. As speculators and hedgers act on available information, their buying and selling activity is reflected in the commodity's price. If the markets are efficient at processing information, today's futures prices are a reasonably accurate estimate of later cash market prices. This is the second major economic function of futures—the competitive determination of commodity prices for later delivery. Often, futures prices are used by businesses to estimate future cash market prices for long-range planning.

Futures Contracts

Futures contracts are *exchange-traded* obligations. The person who goes **long** (that is, who purchases a futures contract) is obligated to take delivery of the commodity at the agreed upon future date. The buyer's maximum potential liability is the full value of the contract.

The person who goes **short** (or sells a futures contract) has taken on an obligation, too—the seller is obligated to deliver the commodity at the agreed upon future date. If the seller does not currently own the commodity, his potential liability is unlimited.

Futures contracts are standardized, and buyers and sellers benefit from the organizations that act as clearinghouses—liaisons between the buyer and the seller—for the contracts. Because of these clearing firms, futures positions can easily be offset prior to delivery. In order to liquidate a futures position without delivering, an investor must enter into the opposite transaction of the one that initiated (opened) the futures position. The offsetting transaction must occur in the same commodity, for the same delivery and on the same exchange. In fact, about 98% of all futures contracts are offset prior to delivery, and in grain futures, the figure is closer to 100%.

Figure 6 illustrates how the volume of futures trading has increased dramatically over the past decade.

Commodity Futures Exchanges

A commodity futures exchange is an organization registered with the Commodity Futures Trading Commission (CFTC) that provides a location (or trading floor) for trading regulated futures contracts.

The term "contract market" is used to refer to that particular exchange designated by the CFTC as the legal location for trading futures contracts for a particular commodity. For example, the Chicago Board of Trade (CBOT or CBT) is the contract market for the soybean complex

FIGURE 6   The Explosion of Futures Trading

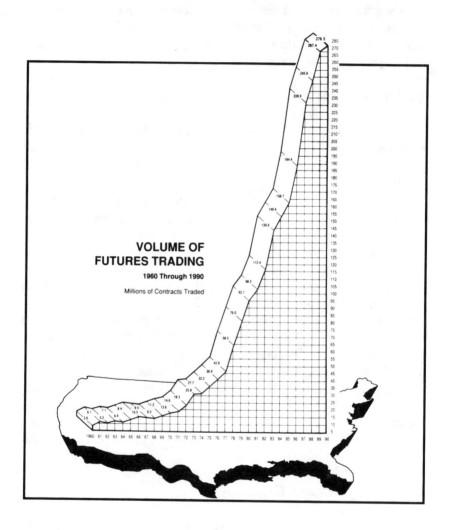

**VOLUME OF
FUTURES TRADING**

1960 Through 1990

Millions of Contracts Traded

Reprinted by permission of the Futures Industry Association.

and T bonds. The New York Mercantile Exchange (NYME) is the contract market for crude oil. The Chicago Mercantile Exchange (CME) is the contract market for pork bellies and the S&P 500. At the CFTC's discretion, more than one exchange can be designated as a contract market for the various commodities.

Clearinghouse

A clearinghouse is an organization that is separate from, but associated with, an exchange (as an example, the CME owns its own clearinghouse). It adds to futures market efficiency by serving as the go-between for the ultimate buyers and sellers of futures contracts. Buyers and sellers of futures contracts rarely have personal contact and do not settle with or deliver directly to each other. Rather, all settlements and deliveries are handled by and through the clearinghouse, making the process much more efficient and less subject to error and disagreement.

Liquidity. A clearinghouse serves to increase the liquidity of the market. It allows investors to establish or offset any futures positions they have taken by buying from or selling to the clearinghouse, rather than having to locate, contact and contract with another buyer or seller directly. Everyone with a position in futures (whether long or short) has a position against a particular clearinghouse rather than directly against another trader. The interchangeability *(fungibility)* of standardized contracts and instruments is a crucial ingredient in the effectiveness of clearinghouses.

Trading. If an investor wishes to take a position in futures, the trade must be executed by a trader who has access to the exchange floor (sometimes the investor is a member and has personal access). The buying customer and the selling customer place orders through their brokerage firms, or futures commission merchants (FCMs). The FCM directs that the trade be executed in the appropriate pit by the floor broker (FB). The FB then confirms the trade to the clearinghouse. If the clearinghouse receives matching confirmations from the floor broker(s) involved in that trade (one on the buy side and one on the sell side), it accepts the position.

Contract guarantor. The buyer has a long position against the clearinghouse's short position, and the seller has a short position against the clearinghouse's long position. In other words, the clearinghouse is the buyer to all sellers and the seller to all buyers.

By stepping between the buyers and sellers, the clearinghouse can act as a guarantor of all outstanding contracts—guaranteeing performance, not delivery. That is, the clearinghouse guarantees that the buyer will receive the monetary value of the position, although it does not guarantee actual physical delivery.

□ SUMMARY

The number and types of securities products have grown as potential areas of profit have been identified. The variety of stocks, bonds, futures and the various derivative securities has been made possible to a large extent by the freedom to trade these products. The trading markets have grown as well to accommodate the vast number of products and transactions. The securities and futures markets today are global, computerized and in operation around the clock. In the next chapter, we will explore the evolution and characteristics of the securities markets.

□ REVIEW

Check how well you have learned the information contained in this chapter by completing the following sentences.

Investors can receive the benefits of diversification, professional management and economies of scale through investments in

_____

(See page 39)

Open-end management companies are more commonly known as

_____

(See page 39)

A company that manages a portfolio of real estate investments in order to earn profits for shareholders is known as

_____

(See page 44)

Businesses organized so that they pass all of their income, gains and losses, and tax benefits directly to their owners are known as

_____

(See page 44)

The purchaser of an option contract has paid money to acquire a

_____

(See page 45)

The seller of an option contract has accepted money and takes on an

_____

(See page 45)

The entity that standardizes option contracts on equities and guarantees their performance is the

---

(See page 47)

A physical good used in business and industry, as well as by consumers, is known as

---

(See page 52)

An important economic benefit of commodity futures trading is

---

(See page 56)

Chapter 4

Securities Markets

"Vigorous financial markets are not the product of desire, or of any one factor. Creation of a trading floor and the installation of computers alone will not ensure a liquid and efficient market. Similarly, while the establishment of a good regulatory structure is important, regulators do not usually create a market. Rather, a combination of factors is needed to establish and maintain strong financial markets, including businesses requiring capital, savings, banking and telecommunications systems, sensible systems of taxation, laws designed to protect against fraud and a judicial system strong enough to protect corporate ownership rights."

Richard C. Breeden, SEC Chairman

Overview

Securities markets have evolved through time from individual securities traders transacting business with other individual traders to a sophisticated, computerized network of global proportions. A single market cannot possibly handle all of the demands for moving capital—particularly as the world moves towards an expanded system of financial trading open 24 hours a day and accommodating trading in equity, debt, currencies, precious metals, commodities, futures and more.

☐ THE NATURE OF SECURITIES MARKETS

A securities market is the location in which or system through which trades of securities occur. The term "Wall Street" is sometimes used to represent the collective marketplace in which employees and customers of the financial industry interact to buy and sell stocks, bonds and other instruments.

When speaking of securities markets, it is helpful to recognize and define the four primary types. Following this brief introduction of these important markets will be discussions of the major players in each of them.

Exchange Market

A securities exchange is a centralized market for securities at or through which buyers and sellers can meet and transact business. An exchange provides its members with certain services, such as standard hours of operation, a trading floor, access to specialists or market makers, minimum standards for listed securities, rules and regulations, an orderly market, electronic quotations and even computerized trading systems. The best known and largest U.S. exchange is the NYSE. Other U.S. stock exchanges include the AMEX and the regional Boston, Cincinnati, Midwest, Pacific and Philadelphia exchanges. In order for securities to be accepted for trading on an exchange, the securities must meet the exchange's listing requirements and are then said to be **listed securities**.

The exchange market is a double-auction market; that is, both buyers and sellers gather on the trading floor of the exchange and shout out bids and offers, competing with each other for securities. Buyers and sellers may be working for themselves (that is, as **principals**) or on behalf of others (that is, as **agents**).

Over-the-Counter Market

The over-the-counter (OTC) market is a decentralized marketplace in which brokers and dealers conduct business by telephone and through computerized quotation systems rather than at a centralized place of business. The OTC is a negotiated market in which buyers and sellers work out prices acceptable to both. The OTC market is also known as the *unlisted market* and handles a majority of the securities issued in this country.

The best known and largest OTC market for stocks is NASDAQ, which is conducted under the auspices of the National Association of Securities Dealers. The "AQ" stands for "automated quotation."

Third Market

The third market is composed of nonexchange member firms trading exchange-listed securities over the counter. The third market had its origins in the 1950s, when it developed as a means for firms to execute large trades of listed securities without using the services, incurring the costs, or being subject to the rules of the exchanges. Many sizable institutional trades (including a significant number of those entered by corporations, money managers and pension funds) are still negotiated and completed in this third market.

Fourth Market

The fourth market consists of direct trading among institutions, professional equities traders, mutual funds, market makers, broker-dealers and others. Those trading in the fourth market are connected and serviced by a computer network developed and operated by INSTINET, a Reuters PLC company. Operating since 1969 as an SEC-registered broker-dealer, INSTINET allows buyers and sellers to negotiate trades directly and anonymously with one another. "Black box" or "screen trading," as it is sometimes called, is becoming an increasingly important market for all types of listed and unlisted securities.

☐ NEW YORK STOCK EXCHANGE

The best known of the national exchanges is the New York Stock Exchange. The NYSE provides a central location at which its members can transact the business of buying and selling securities. The purpose of the NYSE is to maintain high standards of integrity among its members, who are governed by a comprehensive set of rules that promote principles of fair trade. The NYSE is governed by a board of 24 directors (12 securities industry members and 12 public representatives) plus the Board's chairman, executive vice-chairman and president.

The NYSE is a private, not-for-profit corporation. To execute trades on the Exchange floor, brokerage firms must be members of the Exchange. Only individuals can be members—that is, only individuals can own the 1,366 seats on the Exchange. In practice, broker-dealer firms often sponsor or lease an individual's ownership of a seat, and these firms are then known as **member firms**.

Registration of employees. All employees of NYSE member firms who regularly perform the duties of a registered representative, securities lending representative, registered trader or direct supervisor of any of these must be registered through their firms with the NYSE. The Exchange can deny registration to unacceptable applicants. Registered representatives who work for a member firm must exhibit high standards of business conduct and integrity, must pass an examination and must have reached the age of majority. The primary function of a registered representative is to solicit orders from clients for the purchase and sale of securities.

As employees of NYSE member firms, registered representatives must sign statements agreeing to abide by certain NYSE regulations. A person who wishes to become a registered representative must provide the Exchange with a complete history of education and employment, as well as other important information. The person must further agree to read the NYSE constitution and regulations and to abide by them.

The NYSE is not only the United States' largest exchange, but could arguably be called the world's principal stock exchange. Three-quarters of all of the exchange-based trades done in the United States are done on the NYSE. The NYSE opens for trading at 9:30 am EST and closes regular auction trading at 4:00 pm EST.

NYSE Listing Requirements

The members of the NYSE meet on the floor of the Exchange to trade securities that have met the listing requirements of the NYSE. The *initial* requirements for any corporation that wants its stock listed on the NYSE are as follows:

- The market value of its publicly held shares must be at least $18 million.

- At least 1.1 million shares must be publicly held.
- 2,000 stockholders must each hold 100 shares or more (2,000 round-lot owners).
- Corporate earnings before federal income tax must be at least $2.5 million for the latest fiscal year and at least $2 million for each of the two preceding years.

Listing requirements have been modified from time to time in the past, and may be modified in the future.

The NYSE Specialist

Qualifications. About one-quarter of the NYSE members are specialists who trade specific stocks assigned to them. Most specialists handle a number of different stocks traded at the same post. The NYSE board of directors provides for an allocation committee that assigns, or allocates, securities to specialist firms on the basis of their ability to keep an orderly market and on their available capital.

For efficiency, several specialists may combine their capital and form specialist units. Most of these units are partnerships or joint accounts. Therefore, the term "specialist" means a member of a specialist firm who is currently on duty.

Market maker. The specialist's primary function is to make a market or to maintain a fair and orderly market in each security in which he is a specialist. This means that the specialist stands ready to buy or sell a round lot of the security (as well as give a quote on that security). The specialist must have enough capital to maintain a substantial position in the security. Maintaining markets through specialists is one of the functions an exchange performs for public investors.

Agent and principal. The specialist is both agent (broker) and principal (dealer). On the floor of the Exchange, specialists can act in two capacities:

- As agents (or brokers' brokers), executing all orders left with them by other brokers. Specialists accept certain kinds of orders from other members (such as limit and stop orders) and execute these orders as conditions permit. For acting in this capacity, the specialist receives a commission from the other broker's firm.

- As dealers (principals), buying and selling for their own accounts. Specialists, as discussed above, buy and sell in their own accounts (as dealers) to make a market in an assigned stock. They are expected to maintain continuous, fair and orderly markets—that is, markets with reasonable price variations.

Trading posts. On the floor of the Exchange are a number of horseshoe-shaped trading posts with video display terminals. Each stock listed with the Exchange is traded at a particular post. At present, the Exchange has 22 posts, each trading about 100 securities. At each post are the specialists, each of whom has been assigned a certain number of issues.

A commission house (floor) broker with a buy or sell order sent down from that firm's registered representatives (customer orders) or his trading department (house account) takes the order to the post designated for that security. Around the post is a crowd interested in the security. The "crowd" may be as small as one specialist or as large as two specialists and a group of interested brokers and dealers. The commission house broker may execute the buy or sell order in this crowd at the best available price, leave the order with the specialist to execute when the price is right or hand the order to a **two-dollar broker** to trade.

If the commission house broker executes the order within the crowd, information is swapped with the broker on the other side of the trade and a confirmation slip is sent to the order room upstairs. If the order is **away from the market** (that is, the price specified by the order has little chance of being accepted in the crowd), the order is given to the specialist, who will hold it in a book until it can be executed in the market. If and when the order is executed, the specialist will send a confirm of the trade back to the firm that originated the order. The commission house broker can also use the services of a two-dollar broker to handle the order. Two-dollar brokers received their name many years ago when they were paid two dollars a round lot to execute trades—nowadays, they receive a negotiated commission based on the dollar value of each trade. Commission house brokers will use the services of the two-dollar broker in a number of circumstances, such as when they are too busy to handle a particular order, when the order is in a stock traded away from the area normally worked or when the market is moving so quickly that more attention needs to be devoted to the stocks in which they specialize.

The specialist's book. A specialist's most important tool is the specialist's book, a record of limit and stop orders the specialist holds for execution. The book's contents are confidential; the entries need not be disclosed by the specialist to anyone except an official of the Exchange. Because of the increasing volume and speed at which transactions are now occurring, more and more specialists are moving towards computerized books and recordkeeping for efficiency.

The entries in a specialist's book represent a record of limit and stop orders placed with the specialist and awaiting execution. Figure 7 illustrates a page from a specialist's book in ALFA Enterprises stock (which would be abbreviated to its three-letter NYSE quotation symbol). The specialist enters buy orders on the left, sell orders on the right.

If someone were to ask the specialist for the quote for ALF, the reply would be "51 1/8 to 1/2." The current quote on a stock includes the highest limit order on the bid (buy) side and the lowest limit order on the ask (sell or offer) side because market orders to buy or sell can be immediately executed at those prices. Stop orders are not included in the quote because no order has been triggered and therefore it cannot be executed. The Raymond James buy stop order for 300 shares at 51 1/4 is an order to buy if the bids rise to 51 1/4, and the Smith Barney sell stop order for 200 shares at 51 3/8 is an order to sell if the offers fall to 51 3/8.

The specialist's current quote can be translated as follows: market orders to buy stock can be immediately executed at 51 1/2; market orders to sell stock can be immediately executed at 51 1/8.

The specialist must always get the best possible price for a limit order—at the limit price or better. At times, a specialist may be prompted to give quotations that take into account factors in addition to the orders listed in the specialist's book. Specialists often compete against other floor brokers trading in the same stock and sometimes against other specialists if a security is actively traded.

The specialist reveals the number of shares available in a current quote (but does not reveal the number of shares or prices above or below the current quote). Upon request, the specialist will provide a quote and size. The ALF quote "51 1/8 to 1/2, 5–9" means 500 shares bid for at 51 1/8 (the book shows buy orders for 100 shares from A.G. Edwards and 400 shares from Prudential Securities) and 900 shares offered at 51 1/2 (the

FIGURE 7   Example of a Page in a Specialist's Book

BUY	ALF	SELL
1 ML		
1 PW	51	
1 AGE		
4 Pru	1/8	
3 Ray James STOP	1/4	
	3/8	2 Smith Barn STOP
	1/2	4 Oppenheimer
		2 Tucker Anthony
		3 Piper
	5/8	
	3/4	2 DWR
	7/8	5 Bear Stearns

book shows sell orders for 400 shares from Oppenheimer, 200 shares from Tucker Anthony and 300 shares from Piper Jaffray). The quote and size (Q&S) are good only for the moment they are given; however, they provide some indication of the current price. The quote and size are from the specialist's book only and may or may not include any indications from the crowd (the floor brokers surrounding the specialist's post).

☐ AMERICAN STOCK EXCHANGE

The American Stock Exchange is a private, not-for-profit corporation, located in New York City. Companies that list their stock on AMEX tend to be of the mid-size category.

The AMEX, once known as the *curb*, is organized and operates in much the same manner as the larger NYSE. To execute trades on the Exchange floor, brokerage firms must be members of the exchange. The AMEX limits its regular memberships to 675 and allows an additional 203 options principal memberships. The AMEX is governed by a board of 25 governors consisting of twelve Exchange members, twelve public representatives and one chair.

Specialists operate as in-person market makers on the AMEX in much the same way as they operate on the NYSE and on other exchanges that employ the specialist system.

AMEX Listing Requirements

The companies listing their stock on the AMEX tend to be smaller and younger than those listed on the NYSE. The *initial* requirements for any corporation that wants its stock listed on the AMEX are as follows:

- The market value of its publicly held shares must be at least $3 million.
- At least 500,000 shares must be publicly held.
- At least 800 stockholders must each hold 100 shares or more.
- The stock must be trading at a minimum price of $3 per share.
- Corporate earnings before federal income tax must be at least $750,000 for the most recent year.

The AMEX opens for trading at 9:30 am EST and closes its auction market at 4:00 pm EST.

☐ REGIONAL EXCHANGES

In addition to the national stock exchanges, there are other stock exchanges that serve the financial community in different regions of the country. These regional exchanges include the Boston Stock Exchange, the Cincinnati Stock Exchange, the Midwest Stock Exchange, the Pacific Stock Exchange and the Philadelphia Stock Exchange.

Regional exchanges trade securities listed on the national exchanges as well as regional or local securities. Listing requirements on regional exchanges often are less stringent than those of the national exchanges.

Quotations from regional exchanges are often combined, as shown in Figure 8.

FIGURE 8 Example of Quotations from the Regional Markets

U.S. Regional Markets

Sales 100s	Stock	High	Low	Close	Net Chg.	Sales 100s	Stock	High	Low	Close	Net Chg.
	Dually Listed Issues Excluded Tuesday, September 13, 1998						**BOSTON**				
						600	CstCarib	5/16	9/32	5/16	+1/32
	PACIFIC					200	LoJack	1 1/16	3	3	- 3/16
4000	BrockCp	1 3/4	1 3/4	1 3/4	- 1/8	2200	PrcOpt	4 5/8	4 1/2	4 5/8	- 1/8
3600	CanSoPt g	2 3/16	2 1/16	2 3/16	...	Total sales .... 2,500,000 shares					
500	CntAr pf	3/16	3/16	3/16	...		**PHILADELPHIA**				
25000	CrysO pf	5/16	5/16	5/16	...	1000	AppldRs	7/16	7/16	7/16	...
500	GldCycl	4 3/4	4 3/4	4 3/4	+3/8	10000	Arlen	5/256	5/256	5/256	-1/256
7700	Imreg	1 3/4	1 1/2	1 3/4	...	1000	Exectel	5 1/8	5	5	- 1/4
3000	MCRP pf	1/2	1/2	1/2	+1/8	3500	Exten	3 1/8	3 1/8	3 1/8	- 1/4
	BONDS					Total sales .... 3,447,000 shares					
69	AFinl 10s99	77	76 1/2	76 1/2	- 1/4		**MIDWEST**				
10	AFinl 12s99	86	85 3/4	85 3/4	+1/2	300	FstMich	10 3/4	10 3/4	10 3/4	...
644	DrPep 15s98	81 7/8	80 5/8	81 3/8	+7/8	1000	GreifBr	35 3/4	35	35 3/4	+1 5/8
2	Empir 9s07	52 1/4	52 1/4	52 1/4	...	Total sales .... 10,618,000 shares					
Total sales .... 6,789,000 shares											

The Boston Stock Exchange

The Boston Stock Exchange (BSE) is the third oldest stock exchange in the United States, after the Philadelphia and New York exchanges. At its beginnings in 1834, the BSE focused on New England-based banks, insurance companies, railroads and manufacturers. By supporting local companies and entrepreneurs, the BSE contributed greatly to the expansion, growth and health of the New England states.

Currently, more than 1,800 equity securities are traded on the BSE, approximately 95% of which are listed on other regional and national exchanges (primarily the NYSE and AMEX). More than 160 securities of smaller companies are listed exclusively on the BSE.

The BSE was the first U.S. stock exchange to provide memberships to foreign broker-dealers, which greatly facilitated the trading of U.S. securities by foreign investors.

The Cincinnati Stock Exchange

With roots that predate the Civil War, the Cincinnati Stock Exchange (CSE), now owned by the Chicago Board Options Exchange, has been operating continuously since 1885. Although the CSE focused in its early years on newly issued securities of Ohio-, Pennsylvania- and Indiana-based companies, it soon expanded its trading to securities of national interest, and now trades many issues listed on other exchanges.

The CSE operates the nation's only automated auction system for unlisted securities—the National Securities Trading System (NSTS). The NSTS is linked to the NASD's Consolidated Quotation System (CQS) and Intermarket Trading System (ITS).

The Midwest Stock Exchange

First organized as the Chicago Stock Exchange in 1882, the exchange listed 82 bonds and 52 stocks on its first day of trading. Early trading focused primarily on issues such as the Atchison, Topeka and Santa Fe Railroad, the First National Bank of Chicago and the Pullman Palace Car Company. In 1949, the Chicago Stock Exchange merged with the St.

Louis, Cleveland and Minneapolis/St. Paul exchanges to form the Midwest Stock Exchange (MSE).

The MSE provides a listed market for smaller businesses and newer enterprises. Today, more than 2,300 issues are traded on the MSE.

The Pacific Stock Exchange

The Pacific Stock Exchange (PSE) is the only SEC-registered stock exchange west of the Mississippi. The predecessors of the PSE included the San Francisco Stock and Bond Exchange (formed in 1882), the Los Angeles Stock Exchange (1899), the San Francisco Curb Exchange (1928) and the Los Angeles Curb Exchange (1928). Among the early issues of these exchanges were a number of mining and oil company stocks, reflecting the growing importance of these companies to the American West.

The west coast exchanges began merging operations in 1934, and the PSE registered as a stock exchange in 1956. In 1957, 540 preferred and common stocks were listed on the exchange. Today, about 1,500 equity securities (approximately 1,300 dually listed and 150 exclusively listed) and 120 options are traded on the PSE.

The Philadelphia Stock Exchange

The oldest stock exchange in the country is the Philadelphia Stock Exchange (PHLX), founded in 1790. Traders and merchants gathered on a street corner in Philadelphia (a prosperous center of business in the new country) to trade the newly issued bank stocks and government bonds. When securities traders began to gather and trade stocks and bonds in New York two years later, an elaborate communications system consisting of light towers and messengers on horseback was set up so that the two groups could communicate.

The Philadelphia Stock Exchange of today would be difficult for those early merchants to recognize. With three trading floors (concentrating on equity securities, equity options and foreign currencies, respectively) and trading in nearly 2,000 equity issues (including approximately 250 exclusively listed on the PHLX), the PHLX has become a center of sophisticated trading technology.

☐ THE NASDAQ STOCK MARKET

The NASDAQ Stock Market is the second largest stock exchange in the United States and the third largest in the world, exceeded only by the New York and Tokyo Stock Exchanges. "NASDAQ" stands for National Association of Securities Dealers Automated Quotations. The NASD, the largest of the U.S. self-regulatory organizations, operates and regulates NASDAQ.

NASDAQ is different from the traditional exchanges in two key aspects: (1) it has no trading floor, but links broker-dealers by a nationwide and international computer network, the NASDAQ System; (2) securities are not traded by single, assigned specialists, but by competing dealers, or market makers. Very active NASDAQ securities, such as MCI, Apple Computer and Microsoft, may have as many as 50 market-making firms competing for order flow. The average NASDAQ security at the end of 1991 had 10.5 market makers.

In 1991, there were 4,700 securities listed on NASDAQ by 4,100 companies. The aggregate market value of the securities was $508 billion. Dollar volume of trading during the year was $694 billion and share volume was 41.3 billion. NASDAQ share volume was 91% of that of the NYSE, and 12 times that of the AMEX.

The NASDAQ National Market System

The 2,700 largest securities are traded in the NASDAQ National Market System (NMS) and are accorded parity of treatment with exchange-listed securities by federal and state regulators. The Federal Reserve Board has ruled that NASDAQ/NMS securities are automatically eligible for purchase in margin accounts, and almost all the states exempt them from state registration because they meet substantial financial and corporate governance standards.

NASDAQ/NMS securities must be SEC registered, which means that their issuers agree to abide by SEC disclosure requirements. Issuers must have, at a minimum, $4 million in net tangible assets, net income of $400,000 in the last fiscal year or in two of the last three fiscal years, and pretax income for the same periods of $750,000. Securities must have a public float of at least 500,000 shares, a $3 million market value of float and a minimum bid of $5.

The minimum corporate governance requirements for NASDAQ/ NMS companies include: two independent directors; an audit committee composed of a majority of independent directors; examination of all related-party transactions for potential conflicts of interest; securing of specific shareholder approval for certain transactions; and no dilution of shareholder voting rights.

In 1991, NASDAQ/NMS securities accounted for $666 billion in dollar volume of trading, or 96% of total NASDAQ dollar volume. They also accounted for $489 billion in market value, or 96% of total NASDAQ market value.

Regular NASDAQ Securities

The 2,000 smaller, regular NASDAQ securities are also SEC registered and, like NASDAQ/NMS issues, are subject to transaction reporting, in which every trade is reported to the NASDAQ System within 90 seconds of execution. However, these securities are marginable only if the Federal Reserve Board specifically rules them to be so, and they are generally not exempt from state registration. By the same token, they do not have to have the corporate governance features required of NASDAQ/NMS companies.

Qualification standards for regular NASDAQ common stocks include $4 million in total assets, $2 million in capital and surplus, a public float of 100,000 shares, $1 million market value of float and a minimum bid price of $3.

NASDAQ International

NASDAQ International is the world's first intercontinental stock market. Every weekday morning, the NASDAQ Central Computer Complex in Trumbull, Connecticut, opens at 3:30 am EST, to coincide with the opening of the International Stock Exchange in London. A transatlantic cable connects Trumbull with a NASDAQ communications node in London, and the workstations of NASDAQ market makers in London are connected to the node. Thus, it is possible for investors in the United Kingdom to trade NASDAQ and other U.S. securities during the entire time that the U.K. markets are open. It is also possible for broker-dealers in the United States to service their U.K. clients all day long.

A Market Based on Technology

As a market based on technology, NASDAQ offers its users a number of advanced automated services; these include the following.

Small Order Execution System

The Small Order Execution System (SOES) is an automated system for processing individual investors' orders by computer, without telephone contact between market makers. The system guarantees executions at the best bid or ask on NASDAQ. A Limit Order File in SOES allows investors to enter orders that are away from the market; when the market reaches or betters an investor's price, the Limit Order File automatically executes the order. The Limit Order File also has a matching capability that allows two investors with matching buy and sell prices to trade with each other without market maker participation.

SelectNet

SelectNet is a facility for processing larger orders than those processed by SOES and also proprietary orders. It permits a firm to shop an order to a number of others via computer, and to negotiate price and size over the computer.

Advanced Computerized Execution Service

The Advanced Computerized Execution Service (ACES) permits a market-making firm to designate a list of order entry firms from which orders in allowable securities, up to specified sizes, will be automatically executed at the prevailing best price on NASDAQ.

Automated Confirmation Transaction

Trades done through SOES, SelectNet and ACES are locked in for clearing purposes; the Automated Confirmation Transaction (ACT) locks in trades negotiated over the telephone. ACT works in two ways: either both parties to a trade can enter their trade details for on-line matching by the system; or the market maker firm enters its version of the trade and the contra party can accept, enter its own version or decline. ACT makes it possible to compare 90% of all NASDAQ trades within minutes after they take place, 95% by the end of the trade day, and the balance the next day.

□ COMPUTERIZED ORDER ROUTING

The computer revolution has not missed the securities trading industry. As the daily volume of shares traded in each market increases, so does the capacity of the market to handle that volume through assorted automated order routing systems.

In addition to the electronic systems developed by each exchange, the specialists on each exchange are linked to the specialists on every other exchange through the Intermarket Trading System (ITS).

New York Stock Exchange SuperDot

On the NYSE, nearly 75% of the orders received each day are processed through a computerized trading and execution system called *SuperDot* (Super Designated Order Turnaround). Broker-dealers use this computerized order routing system to choose the destination of an order and the route that order will take. An order can be routed directly to the appropriate specialist at his trading post on the floor of the Exchange, or it can be sent to the brokerage firm's house booth for handling by the Exchange member (the **commission house broker**) who represents the broker-dealer. Once the order is received by the specialist or commission house broker, the order is presented in the auction market. If the order is executed, the specialist or commission house broker uses the same automated routing system to send an execution report back to the firm that submitted the order. The broker-dealer then notifies the registered representative, who notifies the customer that the order was executed. Orders executed through SuperDot are often confirmed back to the broker in less than 60 seconds.

All types of orders can be sent to a market through computerized systems, including equity, market, limit, odd lot and options orders. These orders can be sent through the system either *preopening* or *postopening*. As orders are received preopening (that is, before the opening of trading on the Exchange that day), they are automatically paired by the computer with other orders and executed at the opening market. Any order that cannot be matched before the opening is given to the specialist to handle. If an order is received postopening, it is sent directly to the specialist post, where that stock is traded and presented by the specialist to the crowd. All NYSE-listed stocks are eligible for trading on SuperDot, subject to certain limits regarding size and market conditions.

Chicago Board Options Exchange ORS and RAES

The Chicago Board Options Exchange (CBOE) uses the Order Routing System (ORS) to collect, store, route and execute public customer (nonbroker-dealer) orders. ORS automatically routes option market and limit orders of up to 2,000 contracts to the CBOE member firm's floor booth, the floor brokers in the trading crowd, the order book official's (OBO's) Electronic Book (EB) or the Retail Automatic Execution System (RAES).

Market orders and executable limit orders of ten or fewer contracts received by ORS are sent to RAES. Customer orders sent through RAES receive instantaneous executions (fills) at the prevailing market quote and are confirmed almost immediately to the originating firm.

American Stock Exchange AUTOPER and AUTOAMOS

The AMEX uses the Automatic Post Execution & Reporting (AUTOPER) system for equity orders and the Automatic AMEX Options Switch (AUTOAMOS) system for options orders. AUTOPER and AUTOAMOS can be used to electronically route day, good till canceled and marketable limit orders from brokers to AMEX specialists and execution reports from the specialists back to the brokers. An important feature of the AMEX computerized order routing systems is that they are touchscreen-based services. Each specialist has a touchscreen terminal at his post on the trading floor. By simply touching the screen, the specialist can execute orders and generate execution reports for brokers.

Pacific Stock Exchange SCOREX

The PSE uses the Securities Communication, Order Routing and Execution (SCOREX) system to handle more than 60% of the trades taking place on both trading floors of the PSE (Los Angeles and San Francisco). As part of the ITS, SCOREX serves the PSE as an automatic link between the national and regional stock exchanges, and quotes on SCOREX are based on quotes from each exchange trading that particular stock or option.

SCOREX is designed to accept all types of orders, including market, GTC and limit orders in both odd and round lots.

Philadelphia Stock Exchange PACE

The nation's oldest stock exchange, the PHLX, developed the PHLX Automated Communication and Execution (PACE) system in 1975 to automatically route and execute orders. PACE is designed to handle market and limit orders of up to 3,099 shares for more than 1,100 actively traded stocks. PACE can provide electronic executions within approximately 15 seconds of order receipt and send confirmations back to the originating broker-dealer in only a few seconds more.

A special feature of PACE is its ability to check quotations on any of the seven U.S. exchanges and guarantee an execution at the best possible quote found on any of those markets, including the American, Boston, Cincinnati, Midwest, New York, Pacific and Philadelphia stock exchanges or the NASD's Intermarket Trading System/Computer Assisted Execution System.

☐ COMMODITIES FUTURES MARKETS

The establishment of standardized commodity trading and an active futures market occurred several years apart, with the incorporation of the

Chicago Board of Trade (CBOT) in 1848 and the first futures transaction taking place there in 1865. Other futures exchanges soon followed, including: MidAmerica Commodity Exchange in 1868; New York Cotton Exchange in 1870; Kansas City Board of Trade in 1871; New York Mercantile Exchange in 1872; Minneapolis Grain Exchange in 1881; Coffee, Sugar & Cocoa Exchange in 1882; Chicago Mercantile Exchange in 1898; Commodity Exchange, Inc. in 1933; and New York Futures Exchange in 1980. Most of these exchanges patterned themselves after the successful Chicago Board of Trade operations.

Commodity futures exchanges serve many of the same purposes as other securities exchanges. Organized as associations of members, futures exchanges provide their members with such services as standard hours of operation, a trading floor, access to specialists or market makers, minimum standards for listed securities, an orderly market, electronic quotations and computerized trading systems. Memberships are limited to individuals, but members can confer the rights of their memberships on other individuals or on corporations with the approval of the exchange.

Futures trading is accomplished on the floor of the exchange through open outcry, and only members are permitted to trade on the floor (or in the *pits* designated for the trading of particular contracts). Brokers can trade for their own accounts (in which case they are sometimes known as *locals*, *scalpers* or *position traders*) or for the accounts of others, either for their own customer list or for the accounts of customers of the member firms with which they are associated.

□ INSTITUTIONAL MARKETS

An institutional investor is a business or other organization that, by virtue of its size or the size of its portfolio, trades securities in large blocks. Banks, pension funds, mutual funds and insurance companies are frequently classed as institutional investors. Institutions have the size, capacity and often the need to trade directly with other owners of securities without going through an exchange or a securities broker.

The institutional market is massive. In 1989, institutional orders represented about 46% of all trades on the NYSE—an average daily volume of 153.6 million shares. In addition, institutions traded an average of $14.5 billion in debt securities during the same period. At the end of

1989, institutions held about 44% of all the equity securities in the United States—assets valued at roughly $1.7 trillion.

Trading between institutions is done through institutional trading desks at most major securities firms. An institutional trader specializes in moving large blocks of securities for these customers. Telephones and computers connect institutional traders directly to traders at other firms and often to the institutions themselves. Institutional traders, because they trade very large blocks of securities, can be sensitive to even small price variations.

☐ THE PRIVATE PLACEMENT MARKET

Private placements are sometimes used as an alternative to a public offering. In addition to being easier to negotiate and arrange, private placements do not require full-scale registration with the SEC, which saves time and expense for everyone. And, because a private placement does not involve sales to the general public (which the SEC is dedicated to protecting from securities fraud and deception), stock or bonds sold under exemption granted in Regulation D of the 1933 act are not subject to sale-by-prospectus-only requirements. This, however, does not relieve issuers and underwriters of private placements of their obligations to make full disclosure of material facts to buyers.

In most private placements, an underwriter arranges for the placement of an issuer's securities with just one corporation or financial institution, or perhaps with a small group of corporate or institutional buyers. Less common—but by no means rare—are private placements in which an issuer's securities are sold to individual investors, generally wealthy people. In the SEC's view, wealthy people can be expected to be experienced investors, capable of intelligent investment decisions (that is, they are considered **accredited investors**). If such skill and experience is lacking, a wealthy investor can afford to hire a **purchaser representative** who has such talent and experience.

In other instances, private placement securities are sold to ordinary investors. This is rare with corporate securities, but not at all rare in the sale of direct participation programs (also known as *limited partnerships*). There are certain restrictions on the number of these *nonaccredited investors* to whom private placement securities may be sold.

Investment letter stock (two-year holding period). The working premise behind private placement securities (which are not covered by a registration statement) is that institutions and sophisticated individuals who normally buy them do so to fill long-term, permanent investment needs. They do not use them for short-term trading purposes, or worse yet, for turnaround resale to the general public (which would be tantamount to making a public offering without filing a registration statement, thus violating the sale-by-prospectus-only rules).

To ensure that private placement securities are retained as long-term investments, the SEC requires each purchaser to sign an *investment letter*. In signing this document, the purchaser attests to the fact that the securities are being acquired as long-term portfolio additions and acknowledges that the securities are not registered with the SEC and cannot be resold for a period of two full years from the date of purchase. Once the two-year blackout on sales is past, the securities can be sold, subject to volume and reporting restrictions during the third year. After three years, these restrictions are lifted.

Legend stock. To further prevent resale of private placement securities, the certificates themselves must carry a legend (printed on the face of each certificate) alerting any future buyers that the securities are restricted and, therefore, not fully liquid. In addition, the transfer agent for the securities is under direction not to transfer (cancel and reregister) the certificates at any point during the first two years.

Accredited Investors

The target market for private placement securities consists of institutional investors, wealthy individuals, or both, who may or may not be affiliates of the issuer. The SEC refers to these accounts as *accredited investors*.

Institutional investors. Investors in this category include banks and other financial institutions, investment companies and portfolio intermediaries, corporate and employee benefit organizations, endowment associations and not-for-profit foundations.

Wealthy individuals (accredited investors). Wealthy investors, in the SEC's view, are those people who have net worth of at least $1 million or have reported income of at least $200,000 ($300,000 in a joint account) and who have a reasonable expectation of reaching the same income this year.

Issuer insiders and affiliates. *Insiders* include officers and directors (if a corporation is issuing the securities in question) or the general partners (if a direct participation program is being sold as a private placement). *Affiliates* include people in position to *exercise control* over the issuing company or other business concern. Power to control may stem from the person's position with a parent or holding company, or the person may be a major investor (or silent partner) in the issuing company or business venture.

Trusts. Any trust with assets of more than $5 million that was not formed solely to purchase this private placement is considered an accredited investor.

Private Placement Market

The private placement market has grown significantly over the past few years. In 1980, $15.7 billion in capital was raised through private placements of securities, of which 88% represented debt financing and 12% equity or ownership capital. By 1989, the private placement market had grown to more than $198 billion.

☐ INTERNATIONAL MARKETS

The United States is home to only a few of the many financial centers in the world. Major financial centers in Europe and Japan have contributed greatly to the creation of a single world financial community. Today, U.S. citizens invest abroad at an ever increasing rate. Foreign investors impact U.S. markets in ways that would have seemed impossible even a decade ago.

What happens in London and Tokyo can have a dramatic impact on U.S. markets, and vice versa. Traders in the United States need to monitor foreign markets closely in order to detect trends and events that will affect the prices of securities around the world.

The market for international securities operates in much the same way as the U.S. OTC market. Traders often talk to one another by phone and negotiate trades directly. When a U.S. customer wishes to trade a security listed on a foreign exchange or when a foreigner wishes to trade a security listed on a U.S. exchange, the dealers work through one another. One dealer will make the trade on the respective market and charge the other dealer a commission. In some cases, larger dealers, both U.S. and foreign, will own seats on major international exchanges. They engage in transactions directly on those exchanges on behalf of their customers.

The world securities market has grown dramatically over the last decade. In 1980, the world equity market totaled about $2.7 trillion. By 1989, that figure had grown to $11.7 trillion, an increase of more than 400%. This increase occurred through the creation of new companies and the growth of existing companies throughout the world. Foreign activity in corporate debt has grown, too. In 1980, foreigners invested a net $2.9 billion in U.S. corporate debt. By 1989, that figure had grown to $19.5 billion.

Major improvements in telecommunications during the 1970s and 1980s made possible this explosive growth in world markets. More sophisticated telephone and computer networks, increased satellite coverage, better news and international reporting and improved courier and document delivery service have all contributed to the phenomenal growth of the global market.

Today's global securities market is a 24-hour-a-day market, connected by computers and telephones. Events in one part of the world impact other markets immediately. It is possible now for the price of a U.S. security to change dramatically even while some U.S. markets are closed. Events in Europe and throughout the world directly impact U.S. interest rates, oil prices and even food prices.

□ SUMMARY

The securities markets of the United States and the world evolved to meet the needs of the investors, regions, products and companies they serve. They have developed into fair, efficient and economical markets for trading securities, and their continued existence serves as a testament to how well they meet those needs.

The next chapter discusses the people and firms that transact business in securities, the types of trades that take place on the various securities markets, and some of the systems that have been created to handle those trades.

☐ REVIEW

Check how well you have learned the information contained in this chapter by completing the following sentences.

The location or system in which securities trades occur is known as

_____

(See page 64)

The trading system used by exchanges where competing bids and offers are shouted out is called

_____

(See page 64)

The number of seats on the NYSE is

_____

(See page 66)

The "curb" was one of the original names of the

_____

(See page 71)

The computer network used by broker-dealers in over-the-counter securities is

_____

(See page 75)

The increasing volume of shares and the speed at which they are traded led to the development of automated

_____

(See page 78)

A business or other organization that trades securities in large blocks is likely to be

_____

(See page 81)

Securities that are sold to an investor directly by an issuer are known as

_____

(See page 82)

Chapter 5

Trading Securities

"Outright speculation is neither illegal, immoral, nor (for most people) fattening to the pocketbook."

Benjamin Graham

Overview

In the last chapter, we discussed the various markets on which securities are traded. Securities have become the basis for capital-raising and investment because they can be traded freely and easily through these securities markets. Billions of dollars' worth of securities are traded daily by large institutional investors, public and private corporations, broker-dealers and individual investors. These trades would overwhelm the ability of the industry to handle them if it had not developed sophisticated methods for handling these trades. This chapter focuses on the details of how individual securities trades occur and on who is involved in those trades.

□ INSTITUTIONAL TRADING

Institutional trading (the trading done by banks, pension plans, mutual funds and so on) has a great impact on securities markets. Trades valued in millions of dollars are common, and trades in the tens and hundreds of millions are not infrequent. In 1989, institutional transactions accounted for 46% of all shares traded on the NYSE. In contrast, retail trading (individual investors, small companies and others) accounted for only 28% of the shares traded on the NYSE for the same period. Trading between members accounted for the balance.

As the number and size of institutional transactions grow, so does the number that takes place off the floors of the exchanges (for reasons of cost, convenience, anonymity and so on). Non-NYSE brokerage firms evolved specifically to meet the needs of the institutions that sought to trade listed securities off the floor of the NYSE—that is, in the third market. These firms traditionally charged very low commissions to institutions (in contrast to the commissions charged to retail investors), more accurately reflecting the real cost of trading large blocks of securities. Most brokerage firms employ professional institutional brokers to service this market.

Institutional trading is normally done by people who are experienced and knowledgeable about the securities and the markets in which they buy and sell. For this reason, it is often felt that institutional investors do not need the protection that securities legislation offers to smaller investors and many securities regulations specifically exempt institutional transactions from their protection.

Many of the transactions entered into by institutional traders involve what are known as **private placements**. Private placements are those sales by an issuer of stocks, bonds, limited partnerships and other securities directly to an institutional account. Because these private securities transactions take place between institutions (which are expected to have enough knowledge and experience to protect themselves against fraudulent and manipulative trading practices), the registration requirements of the Securities Act of 1933 do not apply. In many cases, other SEC regulations are waived as well where institutional traders are concerned.

Institutions also trade among themselves without using the services of brokers at all, frequently using INSTINET (the fourth market). The terms of these trades are often negotiated directly by the traders at the institutions and take place with no commissions and limited regulation.

□ FIRM TRADING

Broker-dealers trade securities among themselves as a normal part of their business operations. They buy and sell securities in the course of managing their own investment portfolios as well as to meet the needs of their customers.

Brokers deal with each other primarily over the telephone and by computer. Most of the business and contracts brokers enter into among themselves are verbal—and the successful conclusion of these numerous transactions and deals is highly dependent on a strict code of ethics and high standards of honor.

Market Makers

Many brokerage firms provide an additional service to investors by *making a market* in one or more securities. As described earlier, these firms are known as **market makers** in the OTC market and as **specialists** on the exchanges.

In the exchange market, specialists act as market makers and stand ready, willing and able to trade in specified securities. In the OTC market there are no exchanges and no specialists, but some OTC firms acting as dealers make markets in certain securities. They keep these securities in their inventories, buying and selling them for their own profit and at their own risk. Because a broker-dealer acting as a market maker is buying and selling for its own account rather than arranging trades, it is acting as a principal in those transactions and not an agent. OTC securities listed with NASDAQ must be traded by at least two market makers (NASDAQ is the nationwide electronic quotation system for up-to-the-minute bid and asked quotations on approximately 4,000 over-the-counter stocks).

Requirements for market makers. In order for a firm (or an individual) to make a market in a particular security, it must meet certain minimum NASD standards. Among these are that the firm (or individual) must:

- be an NASD member;
- meet minimum net capital requirements;
- be able and willing to execute a trade for at least a normal trading unit at its quote;
- ensure that its quotations are reasonably related to the current market for that security;
- file daily volume reports for those securities in which it makes a market; and
- perform these functions during normal business hours.

When more than one firm makes a market in a security, the market price of that security results from competition among those firms. A registered representative who takes a client's order to buy an OTC stock turns the order over to the trader of the firm, who may contact several market makers and arrange the trade at the lowest offering price.

☐ RETAIL TRADING

The image most people have of the securities industry is that of a representative of a broker-dealer giving investment advice and transacting business with a customer. In many respects, this relationship is the core of the securities business, and the responsibility for building and maintaining this business belongs to the firm's registered representatives.

The broker-customer relationship is critical to the success of the industry and is protected by industry practices and regulations as well as the policies and procedures of each firm in the business.

Prospecting

The process of locating potential customers, qualifying those customers, introducing oneself as a financial professional and initiating a relationship of trust with those potential customers is called *prospecting*. Many brokerage industry professionals would agree that this is the single most important step to building a career as a registered representative.

In developing a prospect into a potential customer, the registered representative must first obtain important personal and financial information about that person. Much of this information can be gathered in the process of opening an account for the person with the brokerage firm. Before a registered representative can begin to discuss investment ideas, time must be spent with the prospect to uncover as much information as possible about his financial position, personal life, investment needs, investment experience, risk tolerance and other areas. Because of the highly personal nature of much of this information, it is critical that both the registered representative and the customer understand that the information will be kept strictly confidential and used only to help choose appropriate investments for the customer's investment portfolio.

Having learned enough about a customer to be able to present an investment idea, the registered representative must judge carefully whether the customer has the ability to understand the investment, the financial resources to commit to the investment, and the willingness to assume the risks of the investment.

Investment Recommendations

If a registered representative's prospecting has been successful and a prospect is willing to become a customer (normally by depositing money into an account or agreeing to enter a transaction), the registered representative needs to have an investment idea appropriate for the prospective customer.

Most of a registered representative's best investment ideas will come from the research department of the brokerage firm itself. Broker-dealers assist their representatives by publishing lists of securities recommendations, analyses and suggestions for their use with customers. These recommendations are developed by the strategists, analysts and other financial professionals the firm employs for just this reason. From among these recommendations (which can include stocks, bonds, municipal and government securities, mutual funds, insurance products and more), a registered representative can usually find an investment that will match closely the goals and needs of the prospective customer.

Customer Investment Outlook

People have many reasons for investing and many needs that must be met by their investments. By asking appropriate questions of customers, the registered representative can uncover these reasons and needs—an important step because customers often do not know why they choose to invest the way they do. Most customers will claim that they invest so that their money will grow. By careful questioning, however, the registered representative may learn that because of tax status, income or other events, some growth investments are appropriate, while others are not.

Transactions

No matter what kind of investment a registered representative has proposed to a customer, there are only two basic transactions that the customer can enter into: buying a security (going *long)* or selling a security. Every securities trade, no matter what the product or how complex the strategy, is a variation of one or both of these two options. The variations, however, are what makes it easy to tailor a particular security transaction exactly to a customer's needs.

Long sale. The most common transaction is the opening or closing of a long position (that is, a position in which a customer buys and pays for securities and then eventually sells those same securities). As an example, a customer decides XYZ stock will appreciate and opens a long position by purchasing shares in the company. In this case, the customer believes the stock's value will appreciate enough to allow sale of the stock at a profit, taking into account commissions and any other costs associated with the transactions. If and when the customer wants to take any profit from the appreciated securities, the long position can be closed by entering an order to sell the securities.

Short sale. Somewhat less typical is the short sale. An investor who sells short has the same profit motive as an investor who buys long, but does everything in reverse. The short-selling investor initially borrows stock from a broker-dealer, then sells the stock at the current market price. The investor anticipates that the price of the stock will go down enough to allow replacement of the borrowed stock at a cheaper price at a later date.

The broker-dealer, if able to find shares of that security to borrow, loans the shares to the client and lets the client take the chance that the stock will indeed become cheaper in the future. The client takes a short position by selling shares of stock he does not own.

Short sales are considered risky. The seller must buy stock to repay the loan and is thus at the mercy of the market. If the stock price rises instead of falling, the investor may have to pay a great deal of money to buy the shares necessary to repay the loan.

Types of Orders

Clients who want to buy or sell securities can enter several types of orders. Following are brief discussions of several of the more commonly used orders.

Market orders. An order that is to be executed immediately without price restrictions or limits is known as a *market order.* It is executed immediately at the current market price. A market order to buy is executed at the lowest offering price available; a market order to sell is executed at the highest bid price available. As long as the security is trading, a market order guarantees execution. No other type of order offers that guarantee.

Limit orders. An order on which a client has placed a limit on the acceptable purchase or selling price is called a *limit order.* Limit orders are usually not executed immediately (unless the price is right). A sell order at a limit sets a minimum price at which the client is willing to sell the stock. The client will gladly accept a higher price than the limit, but not a lower one. A limit order to buy sets a maximum purchase price. The client prefers to buy at the lowest possible price, but will under no circumstances pay more than the limit price.

Stop orders. A stop order (also known as a *stop loss order)* is designed to protect a profit or prevent further loss if the stock begins to move in the wrong direction. The stop order becomes a market order once the stock trades at or moves through a certain price, known as the *stop price.* Stop orders at stock exchanges are usually left with and executed by the specialist. There is no guarantee that the executed price will be as favorable as the stop price. In this way, a stop order differs from a limit order, which does guarantee execution at the limit price or better.

Stop limit orders. A stop limit order is a stop order that, after being triggered, becomes a limit order rather than a market order. For example, an order that reads "Sell 100 XYZ at 52 stop, 51 1/2 limit" means that the stop will be activated at or below 52. Ordinarily, the order then becomes a market order, and shares are sold at the next available price.

However, because there is a 51 1/2 limit, the order to sell cannot be executed at less than 51 1/2. In essence, the investor is saying, "If the stock price goes down, I'd like to get out; but if it goes too far, I'd just as soon hang on until it comes around again."

Again, the execution takes the following order. First the stop is triggered. Then the trade is treated like any other limit order that must be executed at the limit price or better.

Special Use Orders

Different types of order procedures have been developed to meet the needs of securities customers. Following are brief descriptions of some of these orders.

- **Day orders.** A day order is valid only until the close of auction trading on the day it is entered by the client.
- **Good till canceled (GTC) orders.** GTC orders, or open orders, are valid until executed or canceled.
- **At-the-opening and market-on-close orders.** At-the-opening orders are executed at the opening of the market. Market-on-close orders are executed at (or as near as possible to) the closing.
- **Not held (NH) orders.** In an NH order, the floor broker has discretion as to the best time and price for executing the trade.
- **Fill or kill (FOK) orders.** In an FOK order, the entire order is filled immediately or is canceled.
- **Immediate or cancel (IOC) orders.** An IOC order is like a fill or kill order except that a partial execution is acceptable.
- **All or none (AON) orders.** An AON order must be executed in its entirety or not at all.
- **After market trading (GTX) orders.** A GTX order is exposed to the "after market" trading session.

A typical order ticket is shown in Figure 9.

FIGURE 9 Typical Order Ticket

1	NEX ☐ BND ☐ OTC ☐ PBW☐ ASE☐			NYSE Spec. Handling		Other	Seq. No. & Off.
2	BUY	SELL	SS	OTHER		Dupe. or Orig. Seq. No.	
3	Quantity	Symbol or Description		Suffix	Price/MKT	Other than LMT/MKT	
4	Add'l info. - GTC - AON - NH - DNR - Cash - etc.				Account Name		
4a	CXL - OR - BUY - SL - SHORT			Price Chg.			
4b	Quantity	Symbol or Description		Suffix			
					Mgr/VP OK _____		
4c	Add'l former order info., if any			Sol. ☐ Unsol. ☐	☐ Phone ☐ Long		
					☐ Letter ☐ Deliver		
					☐ Person ☐ Convert		
5	Office	Account No.		AE No.	☐ Power ☐ Borrow		
					☐ Other ☐ COD/DVP		
ALFA Financial Services, Inc.				Entered by:			Date:

☐ MONITORING TRADING

The activities of members of the national exchanges are regulated by the act of 1934. Specialists on the exchanges are limited in their activities. Specialists must keep the contents of their books confidential—only a few select officials of the exchange can see the contents.

Broker-dealers may effect a particular transaction either as a **broker** (an *agent* that buys and sells on behalf of others) or as a **dealer** (a *principal* that buys and sells on its own behalf). They may act as either, but not both, in the same transaction. They cannot charge both a markup and a commission in the same trade. Any trading practice that manipulates the market or deceives the investing public is a violation of SEC regulations.

Trading on all exchanges and in all markets is monitored. This monitoring is performed by the exchanges themselves, by the NASD for OTC markets, and by the SEC overall. Regulators are watchful for any trading patterns that could indicate the use of inside information, or other trading activities that would tend to make the markets unfair to other investors.

Trades are monitored in a number of ways. Firms are required to review their customer accounts and report unusual activity to the appropriate regulatory agency. Compliance departments in broker-dealer firms review unusually large trades, large positions in a single security, high levels of trading (which could indicate **churning**, the entering of excessive trades in a customer's account to generate commissions) and any accounts with trades that do not settle on time. All of these situations could indicate that traders are using the markets in a way that renders it unfair to other investors.

Industry regulators can use information of this type to initiate investigations into the activities of firms and individuals. If they detect infractions of the regulations, appropriate action can be taken to correct the situation. That action can include fines, legal action, loss of the broker's license and even jail terms if the infraction is significant. In most cases, trades made in contravention of the regulations are reversed where possible, or compensation is paid to the party suffering the loss.

□ CONSOLIDATED TAPE

The Consolidated Tape system (also known as the **Consolidated Ticker Tape**) is designed to deliver real-time reports of securities transactions to subscribers as they occur on the various exchanges. Subscribers to the Tape can choose to receive transaction reports in either of two ways: over the high-speed electronic line (directly linked to their market information systems); or through the low-speed ticker (visible report) line—the type of report commonly seen as quotes racing across a sign in a brokerage office or at the bottom of the screen on some televised financial programs.

The Tape distributes reports over two different networks that subscribers can tap into through either the low-speed or the high-speed line. Network A reports transactions in NYSE-listed securities (stocks, warrants, rights and so on) wherever they are traded. As an example, a transaction involving NYSE-listed IBM that occurs on the Pacific Stock Exchange will be reported on Network A. Network B carries reports of AMEX-listed securities transactions as well as reports of transactions in regional exchange issues that *substantially meet* AMEX listing requirements. Transactions in these securities must be reported within 90 seconds for inclusion on the Consolidated Tape.

NASDAQ transactions are reported separately in a similar manner.

How to Read the Consolidated Tape

Market identifier. The Tape prints volumes and prices of securities transactions within seconds of their execution on the floor of the NYSE and other exchanges. On the high-speed line, the transactions are reported with a market identifier, a letter identifying the exchange or market on which the transaction took place. Market identifiers are deleted for transactions sent over the low-speed line. The market identifiers currently used on the high-speed line are shown in Figure 10.

Quotations and administrative messages. The Tape reports a variety of information concerning transactions. The ticker abbreviation (trading symbol for the stock, warrant, right and so on) appears on the upper line of the Tape. The number of shares sold, the price and any other necessary information are printed on the lower line of the Tape, immediately below the trading symbol.

Number of shares. The Tape reports a sale of a single round lot (100 shares) of stock by listing the trading symbol and the price at which the transaction occurred but with no quantity (a report of "WX18 1/4" means that 100 shares of Westinghouse Electric were sold at $18 1/4). Sales of multiples of a round lot (200, 900, 1,200 and so on) are indicated by printing the number of round lots followed by the letter "s" and the price (a report of "T2s25" indicates that 200 shares of American Telephone and Telegraph were sold at $25).

FIGURE 10   Market Identifiers in Use on the High-speed Line

AMEX	A	Boston	B	Cincinnati	C
Midwest	M	NYSE	N	INSTINET	O
Pacific	P	NASD	T	Philadelphia	X

FIGURE 11   Trades as Reported on the Tape

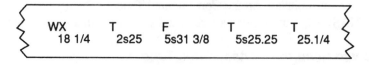

The first three transactions listed on the Tape in Figure 11 (reading from left to right) show trades of 100 shares of WX (Westinghouse Electric) at $18 1/4, 200 shares of T (AT&T) traded at $25, followed by 500 shares of F (Ford) at $31 3/8.

If two similar trades for the same security occur consecutively, the report prints them under the same trading symbol and separates them with a dot. The transaction "T5s25.25" on the Tape in Figure 11 indicates trades of 500 shares of AT&T at $25, followed by 100 shares at $25. The "T25.1/4" indicates two 100-share trades of AT&T, one at $25 and one at $25 1/4. The dot also can indicate that one trade has been split, such as might occur if a sell order for 200 shares were bought by two different brokers.

□ SUMMARY

Securities markets operate on the cutting edge of investment and technological innovation. New ways of doing business continually replace or modify old ways. Despite innovation and progress, however, there is no change in the primary purpose of the securities markets—that of providing issuers and investors with fair, safe and efficient places in which to transact investment business. Therefore, as securities markets have evolved, so have the regulations under which they operate. The next chapter focuses on the history of securities regulation and the way in which it adapts to the changing marketplace.

☐ REVIEW

Check how well you have learned the information contained in this chapter by completing the following sentences.

Institutional traders that do not need the services of a broker-dealer often place their fourth-market trades through

_____

(See page 90)

A broker-dealer that stands ready, willing and able to trade in a specific security, buying and selling for its own account, is most likely

_____

(See page 91)

The process of locating potential customers, qualifying those customers and initiating a relationship with them is known as

_____

(See page 92)

Most of a registered rep's best investment ideas will come from the firm's

_____

(See page 93)

Before entering an initial trade, it is critical that a registered rep determine the customer's

_____

(See page 93)

Buying a security is also referred to as

_____

(See page 94)

An order that is to be executed immediately without limits or special instructions is most likely to be a

---

(See page 95)

Chapter 6

Securities Regulation

"Many objections to laws arise from the impossibility of making them apply only to the other fellow."

Anon

Overview

The U.S. securities industry is among the most highly regulated industries of any kind in the world. Regulation occurs at four levels: federal laws and rules; state laws and rules; rules of the exchanges and other self-regulatory bodies; and standards that firms impose individually on themselves. The overriding purposes of securities regulation are to protect investors and to provide safe, efficient markets in which capital can be raised. The effectiveness of this regulatory tapestry has contributed greatly to the evolution and advancement of securities markets in the United States.

☐ THE HISTORY OF REGULATION

Prior to the great stock market crash of 1929, there was no federal regulation of the securities industry. As the excesses of the pre-crash period came to light in the early 1930s, two key legislative acts were developed to regulate the industry. These were the Securities Act of 1933 and the Securities Exchange Act of 1934. These two acts established the regulatory framework that still governs the industry today. The purpose of these legislative packages is to protect investors by requiring proper disclosure of information and establishing procedures that safeguard against fraud, misrepresentation and manipulation.

Other regulatory acts were passed during the next decade, including the Maloney Act, the Trust Indenture Act of 1939 and the Investment Company Act of 1940. As the securities industry grew, especially through the 1960s and 1970s, new financial products were developed. With every new investment product came changes and additions to the regulatory guidelines.

In the early 1980s, "deregulation" became the watchword of the federal government. More financial products were introduced, and the industry was encouraged to regulate itself even more than it already did. Throughout the 1980s, capital markets grew rapidly.

This rapid expansion of capital markets caused a realignment of the financial firms of the day. Many of the firms that dominated the industry prior to 1980 looked radically different by 1990. A few firms and individuals abused their near monopoly of markets or access to information. The financial collapse of certain markets (such as junk bonds), episodes of sharp gyrations in the markets and the improper but highly publicized acts of a handful of individuals caused the industry to reaffirm the need for stronger regulatory controls.

An increased emphasis on regulatory vigilance was evidenced through actions by government, the courts and regulatory bodies. In October 1990, the federal government introduced the Market Reform Act of 1990. The act allows the Securities and Exchange Commission to regulate computerized trading. It also increases the authority of the SEC to shut down securities markets in times of market emergency.

The U.S. Justice Department has followed up on civil securities cases with criminal actions on a more regular basis, and the SEC and compliance departments of member firms are becoming ever more active and vigilant in regulating trading practices.

☐ FEDERAL REGULATION

The basis of all federal regulation in the securities industry is to be found in the Securities Act of 1933 and the Securities Exchange Act of 1934. These two acts established the regulatory framework that still governs the industry. This framework is illustrated in Figure 12.

FIGURE 12   Regulatory Framework of the Securities Industry

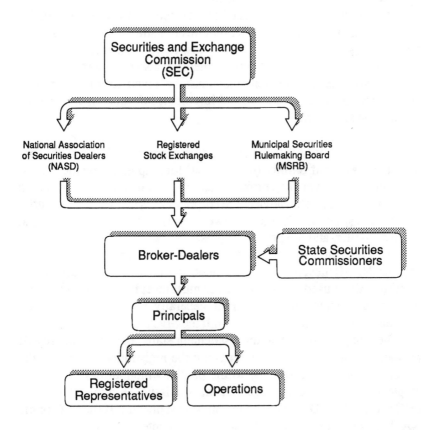

The Securities Act of 1933

The Securities Act of 1933 regulates new issues of corporate securities sold to the public. The act is also referred to as the *Full Disclosure Act*, the *New Issues Act*, the *Trust in Securities Act* and the *Prospectus Act*. It requires a company, with certain exceptions, to file a registration statement with the Securities and Exchange Commission (SEC) before it can sell a new issue of debt or equity securities to the public. The registration statement includes information regarding the financial history of the firm, its management practices and other information of interest to potential investors.

The main purpose of the act is to ensure that the investing public is fully informed about a security and its issuing company when the security is first sold to the public. This act requires registration of new issues of nonexempt securities with the SEC (most exempt securities are issued by municipalities and the U.S. government). It also requires the issuance of a **prospectus**, a document that must be given to all prospective purchasers containing much of the important information filed in the registration statement.

Raising capital. When a corporation needs capital, it usually contacts an **investment banker** (underwriter) for help in raising the money. The underwriter (usually a broker-dealer firm with experience in selling new issues to the public) advises the corporation as to the type of security to issue. An agreement is signed between the issuer (the corporation) and the underwriter, and the process begins.

The issuer of a security files a registration statement with the SEC and the NASD describing its business and how the proceeds of the offering will be used. While the issuer must meet the registration statement requirements, the underwriter generally writes the registration statement and files the paperwork with the SEC and the NASD.

The filing of the registration statement starts a 20-day **cooling-off period.** For at least 20 days after filing the registration statement, the issuer cannot sell the security to the public, which allows the market ample time to consider and evaluate the new issue. During this time, the SEC and the NASD review the registration statement. If the SEC or the NASD has questions about the statement's content or completeness, it interrupts the cooling-off period by sending a **deficiency letter** to the underwriter. Delays caused by deficiency letters are an expected part of an underwriting, so the cooling-off period for a new issue can last considerably longer than 20 days.

The SEC reviews the statement only for completeness. It does not approve, disapprove or in any other way comment on or judge the merit of the securities, and this fact must be displayed prominently on the front of the prospectus. The primary focus of the NASD's review concerns the underwriter's compensation and any conflicts of interest it may have with the issuer.

When the SEC and the NASD are satisfied with the completeness and content of the registration statement, the new issue is released for sale to the public. A new issue must be registered in each state in which the underwriter wishes to sell the securities.

Antifraud Provisions

Although a security might be exempt from the registration requirement (and regulations regarding disclosure of information), no offering is exempt from the antifraud provisions of the Securities Act of 1933. The antifraud or antimanipulation provisions of the act of 1933 apply to all new securities offerings, whether exempt from registration or not. Issuers must provide accurate information regarding any securities offered to the public.

The Securities Exchange Act of 1934

After the Securities Act of 1933 was enacted regulating primary issues of securities, attention turned to the need for regulation of secondary trading. The primary intent of the authors of the Securities Exchange Act of 1934 was to enact legislation that would ensure a fair and orderly market for the investing public. The act achieves this goal by regulating the activities of the securities exchanges and the OTC market. Also known as the *Exchange Act*, the act of 1934 established the SEC and gave the SEC the authority to regulate and oversee the securities markets and to register and regulate the exchanges.

The Securities Exchange Act of 1934 also required the registration of several other entities with the SEC, including exchange members and broker-dealers that trade securities either OTC or on an exchange and individuals who effect securities trades with the public.

In summary, the Securities Exchange Act of 1934, which has much greater breadth than the act of 1933, addressed, among other things, the following:

- creation of the SEC
- regulation of exchanges
- regulation of credit by the Federal Reserve Board
- registration of broker-dealers
- regulation of insider transactions, short sales and proxies
- regulation of trading activities
- regulation of client accounts
- regulation of the OTC market

Regulation of the securities industry was further refined by legislation that expanded or amended the acts of 1933 and 1934. Following are some of the more important pieces of this evolving legislation.

The Securities and Exchange Commission

The SEC, created by the act of 1934, was given responsibility and authority to regulate the securities markets. The SEC is made up of five commissioners appointed by the President of the United States and approved by the Senate. One of the primary responsibilities of this group is to enforce the act of 1934.

The SEC has established rules regarding net capital requirements for broker-dealers, hypothecation of customers' securities (lending them as collateral for a loan), commingling of broker-dealer securities with those of customers, the use of manipulative and deceptive devices and broker-dealer recordkeeping. The SEC enforces the Securities Exchange Act of 1934 (and others) by providing rules and prescribing penalties for violations.

Registration of Exchanges and Firms

Registration of exchanges. Under the 1934 act, the national securities exchanges must register as such with the SEC. When they register, the exchanges agree to comply with and help enforce this act and to institute and enforce disciplinary procedures for members that do not adhere to just and equitable trade practices. Each exchange supplies the

SEC with copies of its bylaws, constitution and articles of incorporation. If the exchange wishes to change or amend its rules at some later date, it can do so only after notifying and, in some cases, receiving the permission of the SEC.

Registration of issuers. In addition to requiring the registration of exchanges, the act of 1934 requires companies that list securities on those exchanges to register with the SEC. Each listed company must file quarterly and annual statements with the SEC disclosing its financial status (as well as other information) to the SEC and to the general public.

Many firms with securities that are traded OTC must also register. Those firms with 500 or more stockholders and assets of $1 million or more are required to do so.

Registration of broker-dealers. Specific broker-dealers must also register with the SEC. Exchange members who do business with the public and any broker-dealer that does business over the counter or uses an instrument of interstate commerce (such as the mail, telephone, television, radio and so on) to conduct over-the-counter securities business must register and file regular reports with the SEC.

There are some exemptions from the requirements to register, including small local exchanges and any broker-dealer that deals strictly on an intrastate basis. An intrastate firm, however, cannot use the mail or other instruments of interstate commerce and still qualify for the exemption from registration.

Regulation of Credit

The act of 1934 empowered the **Federal Reserve Board (FRB)** to regulate extensions of credit and the time frames for payment of same. Maintenance requirements for margin accounts are set by the various self-regulatory organizations (NYSE, NASD and so on). The FRB enforces the following regulations covering the extension of credit for securities purchases:

- **Regulation T**—regulates the extension of credit by broker-dealers;
- **Regulation U**—deals with the extension of credit by banks;

- **Regulation G**—deals with the extension of credit by other than commercial banks or broker-dealers; and
- **Regulation X**—deals with the credit obtained to purchase, carry or trade in nonexempt securities.

Other Federal Regulations

Glass-Steagall Act (Banking Act) of 1933

Following the crash in 1929, Congress concluded that one factor in the general financial collapse was the fact that commercial bankers engaged in investment banking. In their role as commercial bankers, they took deposits and financed commercial enterprises. As investment bankers, they underwrote stocks, using deposits to finance their securities ventures. Losses on the investment side of the bank, therefore, affected the health of the commercial operations and the safety of depositor funds.

With the Glass-Steagall Act (Banking Act) of 1933, Congress attempted to erect a wall between commercial and investment banking. The act forbids commercial banks to underwrite securities (except municipal general obligation bonds) and denies investment bankers the right to open deposit accounts or make commercial loans.

In the 1980s and 1990s, the Glass-Steagall Act has been reexamined and its application to the current securities and banking industries questioned. Banks now offer many investments that were once the sole province of investment bankers, including money-market funds, discount brokerage services, commercial paper and other investment services. Glass-Steagall will continue to evolve as the banking and securities industries seek new ways to ensure profitability while continuing to protect the interests of investors.

Maloney Act

As a 1938 amendment to the act of 1934, the Maloney Act provided for the creation and registration with the SEC of a national securities association to regulate brokers and dealers not affiliated with an exchange (that is, the OTC market). Under the provisions of this amendment, the NASD was created. It is the only organization of securities dealers registered with the SEC under this act.

The primary force behind the Maloney Act and the formation of the NASD was the recognition of the securities industry itself of the need for self-regulation. The NASD was created to provide standards and guidelines for the industry and to encourage industry self-discipline and self-regulation. The formal purposes of the NASD are to promote the securities business, standardize business practices, encourage high standards of honor and encourage self-discipline among member firms. To meet these goals, the NASD has adopted the **Rules of Fair Practice**, which promote just and equitable principles of trade.

Trust Indenture Act of 1939

The Trust Indenture Act of 1939 was written as a means of providing information and protection to the buyers of corporate and other debt securities. The act specifically requires that corporate bond issues of more than $2 million and with a maturity date more than nine months in the future be issued with a **trust indenture** (a document containing the agreement between the corporate issuer and the investors). The trust indenture contains *covenants* (promises) that serve to protect the bondholders, such as the promises to send bondholders semiannual financial reports and make periodic filings with the SEC showing that the company is in compliance with the provisions of the indenture. The trust indenture is usually a very large document, making it difficult to send a copy to each investor. Investors are, however, always entitled to review a copy at the custodian bank, where it is usually held.

Investment Company Act of 1940

The purpose of the Investment Company Act of 1940 is to regulate investment companies in order to ensure that they adhere to specific rules and regulations and to keep investors fully informed about investment company operations. The act regulates the issuance of investment company securities by setting standards for the organization and operation of investment companies, the pricing and public sale of the investments and compliance with reporting requirements.

The act of 1940 is administered by the SEC, and investment companies that wish to sell their shares publicly must register with the SEC.

Investment Advisers Act of 1940

This act requires that if a person is in the business of giving investment advice (that is, the person actually gives such advice and charges a fee for the advice), the person must register as an investment adviser.

Securities Investor Protection Act of 1970

The Securities Investor Protection Corporation (SIPC) was established in 1970 with the passage of the Securities Investor Protection Act. The purpose of the act is to protect the customers of securities firms that file for bankruptcy. SIPC was formed as a nonprofit corporation, not as a government agency like the Federal Deposit Insurance Corporation (FDIC). SIPC members include all broker-dealers registered under the Securities Exchange Act of 1934, all members of national securities exchanges and most NASD members.

If a securities firm that fails is unable to return the assets of its customers, SIPC provides protection to each customer for up to $500,000 for cash and securities at the firm, with a limit of $100,000 on the cash portion. SIPC derives its resources mainly from assessments on its members.

Securities Acts Amendments of 1975

The Securities Acts Amendments of 1975 established the Municipal Securities Rulemaking Board (MSRB). The MSRB writes the rules pertaining to the issuance and trading of municipal securities. The MSRB does not enforce the rules that it makes, however. The SEC, FRB and NASD provide the MSRB with enforcement assistance.

Insider Trading and Securities Fraud Enforcement Act of 1988

The Insider Trading and Securities Fraud Enforcement Act of 1988 expanded the definition of and the liabilities and penalties for the illicit use of *material nonpublic* information. Insiders may now be held liable for more than just transactions in their own accounts. The act recognizes the fiduciary responsibility of the insider to the issuer, the stockholders and others who might be affected by trades made with insider knowledge.

Investors who have suffered monetary damage because of insider trading now have legal recourse against the insider and any other party who had control over the misuse of nonpublic information.

An insider is any person who has access to nonpublic information about a corporation. Insiders may not use inside information as a basis for personal trading until that information has been made public. The SEC can levy a penalty of up to three times the amount of profit made (or loss avoided) if inside information is used. Any individual who is a corporate insider and owns securities in that corporation must file a statement of ownership with the SEC.

□ STATE SECURITIES REGULATIONS

In addition to federal securities regulations, each state has laws that pertain to the issuance of securities and to the trading of securities in the secondary market. State securities laws are known as **blue-sky laws**. The term "blue-sky" was used by a Kansas Supreme Court justice, who referred to "speculative schemes that have no more basis than so many feet of blue sky." The Uniform Securities Act serves as model legislation that each state may follow or adapt to its own needs.

Most states require broker-dealers that do business in a particular state to register with that state's securities commission. Salespeople (agents) associated with a broker-dealer also must be registered in the state(s) where they do business. In most states, securities, too, must be registered in the state before they can be sold to the public.

Several states require that broker-dealers have a minimum amount of net capital in their businesses. In many states, broker-dealers must post fidelity bonds. The state securities administrators have the power to revoke the registration of a broker-dealer or the license of a registered representative if the firm or representative has violated any of that state's securities laws.

☐ SELF-REGULATORY ORGANIZATIONS

The self-regulatory organizations (SROs) governing the securities industry fall into two groups—the securities exchanges and the organizations established solely for the purpose of self-regulation.

The Exchanges

All stock exchanges act as self-regulatory bodies. Most exchanges base their rules and practices on those of the NYSE, which developed its rules to promote ethical conduct of members and fair trading practices.

The NYSE regulates its members through the registration of member employees, the establishment of standard trading practices and the development of minimum standards of business practice.

Registration of Member Employees

Registration of employees of NYSE members allows the NYSE to set minimum standards of conduct and education. To represent a member firm in dealing with the public, an individual must pass qualifying examinations and have reached the age of majority. The NYSE requires the member firm to investigate the business practices of prospective employees as well to ensure a high level of ethical conduct.

Registered representatives must be full-time brokers—part-time association is permitted only where that association is not contrary to the public interest (as an example, an assistant to a registered representative may be registered without intending to build a full-time business). A person who wishes to become registered with the NYSE must sign a statement agreeing to abide by the regulations of the Exchange.

The National Association of Securities Dealers

The NASD was formed when the securities industry recognized the need for an organization that would provide standards and guidelines for the industry and also self-discipline. The purposes of the NASD are to promote the securities business, standardize business practices, encourage high standards of honor and instill self-discipline among member firms. The NASD has adopted the Rules of Fair Practice, which promote just and equitable principles of trade in order to protect investors.

To fulfill its role as a self-regulatory organization, the NASD has outlined its policies in the *NASD Manual*. The manual describes the following four sets of basic rules and codes by which the OTC market is regulated:

1. **Rules of Fair Practice.** This sets out fair and ethical trade practices that must be followed by member firms and their representatives when dealing with the public.
2. **Uniform Practice Code.** This establishes the *Uniform Trade Practices*, including settlement, good delivery, ex-dates, confirmations and other guidelines for broker-dealers to follow when they do business with other member broker-dealer firms.
3. **Code of Procedure.** This describes how the NASD hears and handles member violations of the Rules of Fair Practice.
4. **Code of Arbitration.** This governs the resolution of disagreements and claims between members, registered reps and the public; it addresses monetary claims, not violations of the Rules of Fair Practice.

Self-registered by virtue of the Maloney Act, the NASD was developed primarily to regulate broker-dealer trading in the over-the-counter market. The NASD is a self-funded organization. It assesses fees against its members' registered representatives and applicants. The NASD has established eleven districts in the United States, with a District Business Conduct Committee (DBCC) to administer NASD rules and regulations in each.

Any person who transacts business in securities as a representative of a firm or as a dealer may also be required to register with the NASD. In addition, qualification examinations are required for those individuals who wish to be representatives or principals of a member firm.

The process of qualification and registration is a lengthy one. It involves extensive disclosure on the part of the member firm. Individuals who register are also required to provide extensive personal details. If an individual has been expelled or suspended by another securities organization or a national exchange, NASD registration may be refused. In addition, if the SEC has suspended or revoked the broker-dealer's license, or if an individual has been convicted of a felony within the previous ten years, registration may be refused.

Municipal Securities Rulemaking Board

The MSRB is an independent self-regulatory organization established by the Securities Acts Amendments of 1975. The act of 1975 requires underwriters and dealers of securities to protect the interests of investors (as well as themselves), be ethical in offering advice and be responsive to complaints and disputes.

The MSRB is headed by a 15-member board: five members represent broker-dealer firms, five members come from the banking industry and five are public representatives. This is the organization that makes rules pertaining to the issuance and trading of municipal securities.

The rulemaking process. In the event the Board determines that it is necessary to revise or amend an MSRB rule, it will publish the proposal in the *Federal Register* and circulate a draft of the rule to the industry for comment. This process also is true for the exchanges and the NASD. During the public comment period, the Board submits the proposed rule change simultaneously to the SEC and the federal bank regulatory agencies for their official review. After the public comments, and with SEC approval, the rule becomes effective.

The Board does not have to seek comments or prior SEC approval on rules that relate solely to the Board's administration or assessments of members. These rules become effective on filing with the SEC (although the SEC still has 60 days to rescind a rule).

Finances. Like the NASD and NYSE, the MSRB is a self-supporting SRO that carries out the wishes of the SEC in all matters regarding municipal securities. Annual fees of $100 charged to each municipal securities dealer, supplemented by fees paid for each municipal bond that is underwritten, provide the funds necessary to run the MSRB.

Rule enforcement. Unlike the NASD and NYSE, the MSRB does not have the authority to enforce the rules it makes. The rules that pertain to broker-dealers are enforced on its behalf by the NASD and SEC, and the comptroller of the currency enforces MSRB rules that pertain to national banks. The Federal Reserve Board enforces MSRB rules governing any nonnational bank that is a member of the **Federal Reserve System**. The Federal Deposit Insurance Corporation (FDIC) enforces MSRB rules for nonnational banks that are not members of the Federal Reserve System.

Because municipal bonds are exempt securities (they are not required to be registered under the act of 1933 with the SEC before issue), neither the MSRB nor the SEC has any authority over municipal issuers. Municipal issuers, underwriters, brokers and dealers are, however, always subject to the antifraud provisions of the act of 1934.

The MSRB regulates the trading of municipal securities through its authority over the broker-dealers and banks that underwrite and trade municipal securities. Municipal issuers, underwriters, brokers and dealers are, however, always subject to the 1934 act's antifraud provisions.

Options Self-regulatory Council

The Options Self-regulatory Council was established in the late 1970s to provide the options industry and the options exchanges with a similar means of self-regulation. The Council is composed of representatives from the CBOE, the NASD and the New York, American, Midwest, Philadelphia and Pacific stock exchanges. One of the primary goals of the Council is to develop guidelines for the uniform regulation of options sales practices that can be used by each options exchange in the establishment of rules and regulations for its own members.

☐ FIRM REGULATION AND COMPLIANCE

Most broker-dealers have compliance departments dedicated to ensuring that the rules developed by the many regulatory bodies are enforced. Compliance officers and managers serve a critical function in a brokerage firm, actively monitoring trading, account management and a host of other areas.

Compliance departments review all of a firm's public communications prior to release, including newsletters and market reports, prepared telephone and speech scripts, newspaper, television and other advertisements, and form letters sent by brokers to their customers, filing copies as necessary with appropriate regulatory authorities.

The NYSE and NASD set minimum standards. Many firms have policies and standards that exceed regulatory minimums. In addition to monitoring compliance with regulatory agencies, compliance departments cover employees' compliance with these internal policies and procedures. People employed in the compliance departments usually have extensive legal or accounting training as well as extensive knowledge of NYSE and NASD rules.

☐ SUMMARY

The U.S. securities industry operates successfully within a highly self-regulatory environment, a claim few other industries can make. This self-regulation has provided this country's corporations and investors with a fair and efficient market in which to trade securities.

Securities trading is a highly visible, important part of the securities industry. Less visible to most investors, but even more critical to the industry, is the investment banking business—the business of issuing securities. The following chapter provides an in-depth view of the processes involved in bringing new issues of securities to market.

□ REVIEW

Check how well you have learned the information contained in this chapter by completing the following sentences.

Full Disclosure Act, Trust in Securities Act and *Prospectus Act* are all names for the

_____

(See page 106)

The filing of a registration statement with the SEC begins a cooling-off period of

_____

(See page 106)

The Securities and Exchange Commission was created by the

_____

(See page 107)

The Securities Exchange Act of 1934 requires the registration of

_____

(See page 107)

The Glass-Steagall Act was designed to separate the activities of

_____

(See page 110)

The Maloney Act permitted the formation of the NASD, which was the nation's first

_____

(See page 110)

The Securities Investor Protection Corporation was established to protect the interests of customers of firms that

_____

(See page 112)

The MSRB was established by the

_____

(See page 112)

State securities regulations are commonly called

_____

(See page 113)

The department in most broker-dealers that performs the internal monitoring and regulatory functions is the

_____

(See page 117)

Chapter 7

Issuing Securities

"In supplying businesses with funding, a securities market must decide 'which entrepreneurs and companies have what it takes to become a success.' "

Richard C. Breeden, SEC Chairman

Overview

In general, securities come to market in one of two ways: as new issues (primary distributions) from a corporation, municipality or federal government or in secondary trades between investors. This chapter introduces you to the market for newly issued securities, beginning with a review of the stock market crash of 1929, the calamity that precipitated the legislation now governing securities issuance and trading. From there, the chapter discusses investment banking and the underwriting process. The difference between primary and secondary offerings, public offerings and private placements, competitive and negotiated bidding are also discussed. Finally, the chapter looks at leveraged buyouts and the role of the investment banker in mergers and acquisitions.

□ THE REGULATION OF NEW ISSUES

The Crash of 1929

During the early 1900s, America enjoyed a long-term bull market that promised to last forever. Attracted by the dream of easy money, Americans turned en masse to Wall Street, poring over stock price tables and learning the language of trading operations. For the first time, the general public became a significant factor in the market; but often they purchased securities knowing little about the issuing company or its plans for spending their money.

Investors borrowed heavily (that is, they bought securities on margin). Doing so was an act of faith in the perpetual bull market and an outcome of generous credit policies that allowed investors to borrow most of the purchase price of stock. By the summer of 1929, more than a million Americans held stock on margin.

The rest is familiar history. Stock prices reached new heights in early September 1929. Then things fell apart. By the third week of September, tumbling prices brought the Dow Jones averages down 19 points. A month later, averages were 50 points below the September high mark. The downward spiral of prices gained momentum, breaking through crumbling layers of anticipated buying support.

Rapidly declining prices meant investors' stocks were no longer adequate security for the loans they had taken out to buy them. Securities purchased on very low margins, therefore, were sold to raise money, and this caused even deeper drops in market prices. Dumping stock for forced sale destroyed grassroots investors and wealthy traders alike, including those supposedly safe investment trusts, which unloaded their holdings for whatever they could bring.

The Legislative Reaction

After the crash, the market continued to decline for several years. During that time, Congress examined the causes of the debacle and passed several laws meant to prevent its recurrence. This legislation included, among other acts, the Securities Act of 1933, the Glass-Steagall Act of 1933 and the Securities Exchange Act of 1934.

The Securities Act of 1933

The 1933 act requires issuers to make full disclosure to the SEC for regulatory surveillance and compliance use. It also requires that much of the same full disclosure of information be made to investors. Disclosure to investors is accomplished through the prospectus, which in large part is the same information supplied in the registration statement.

The registration statement and prospectus requirements under the 1933 act apply to both new issue and additional issue securities and to offerings being made by the issuing corporation (primary offerings), as well as by selling stockholders (secondary offerings), or by both.

SEC's Role in Reviewing Registration Statements

The information supplied to the SEC becomes public information (accessible to anyone) once a registration statement is filed.

SEC approval. Although the SEC neither approves nor disapproves of the securities covered in a registration statement (based on the investment merits and quality of the issue), the Commission does inspect each registration statement for omissions of material facts, clarity of information and all supporting financial documentation.

Amendments and stop orders. If the SEC is not satisfied with the completeness of the information contained in a registration statement, it will issue a deficiency letter, delaying the effective date until satisfactory amendments have been filed. Or, if the Commission is of the opinion that flagrant omissions of material facts exist, it will issue a *stop distribution order* suspending or denying registration, which may kill the underwriting entirely.

Effective date in 20 calendar days. In the absence of a deficiency letter or stop order, a registration statement becomes effective 20 calendar days from the date of filing.

Securities exempt from registration under the 1933 act. Not all securities issued and traded are subject to the disclosure requirements of the act of 1933. Securities exempt from registration include:

- U.S. government securities
- state and municipal bonds
- commercial paper and bankers' acceptances (less than 270 days)
- national and state bank securities (except bank holding companies)
- building and loan (S&L) securities
- any interest in a railroad equipment trust

Trust Indenture Act of 1939

The Trust Indenture Act of 1939 was created, in part, to provide the same sort of protection to the purchasers of debt securities as is afforded to investors in equities. The term "debt securities" includes all notes, bonds, debentures and other similar evidences of indebtedness. The term "trust indenture" covers any mortgage, trust or other indenture, or any similar instrument or agreement.

As its major focus and means of protecting the public interest, the act prohibits the sale of any debt security unless it has been issued under a trust indenture. In addition to requiring full disclosure about the nature of the debt issue and the issuer, the trust indenture identifies the rights and powers of the trustee, as well as the trustee's responsibilities.

☐ INVESTMENT BANKING

Investment banking firms serve corporate business as a primary source of long-term capital. These long-term capital needs range from initial formation of capital for new business ventures to expansion capital for established corporations. Investment bankers (most of which are securities broker-dealers as well as investment bankers) also play major roles in converting privately owned companies into publicly held corporations, wherein stockholders in the privately held firms sell some or all of their ownership interests to the public.

Corporations raise capital by issuing *investment securities* (equity, debt or both), which are then sold to an investment banker in exchange for the needed cash. Using the firm's own money, the investment banker acquires the issuer's securities and either holds them in a proprietary investment portfolio (which is what investment bankers did in the past as a matter of routine) or immediately resells the securities to individual and institutional investors in a public offering (which is what most investment bankers do today).

Issuance markets. The new issue market consists of companies "going public"—privately owned businesses raising capital by selling common stock to the public for the very first time. New issue securities are also known as *initial public offering (IPO)* securities.

The **additional issue market** is made up of securities issues from companies that are already publicly owned (that is, they already have stock outstanding with the public). These companies are now raising additional funds by issuing more stock or by issuing bonds. This is accomplished when an underwriter either distributes the securities in a public offering or arranges for the shares or bonds to be sold in a private placement.

In 1991 alone, U.S. corporate underwritings distributed to the public amounted to $583.1 billion, and private placements of corporate securities amounted to almost $118 billion. At the same time, municipal issues in the United States amounted to $170 billion, and the U.S. government issued $435 billion in new securities. Add to these numbers the $99 billion in mergers and acquisitions and you can begin to grasp the size of the investment banking needs in the United States.

Corporate Information Gathering

The investment banker that helps a corporation bring a new issue to market must do a considerable amount of preliminary study and work. It is essential that the company's financing proposal be studied carefully to determine whether it is appropriate in this capital-raising situation, or whether an alternative would be more suitable. Verification must be made of the issuing corporation's financial position and business operations. The legality of the issue as it is proposed must be determined. The investment banker must investigate the company's industry and how the firm fares in that industry, as well as how its various departments (such as research and product development) are addressing changes in their industry, markets and competition. And just as importantly, the investment banker must determine how well the company handles its own working relationships with its managers and employees—by looking at such issues as employee turnover, labor structure, morale and so on.

In addition to these preliminary studies, much information must be gathered to meet the registration statement and prospectus requirements, and to satisfy the underwriter's own need for concrete facts and figures in support of the decision to proceed with the underwriting.

Due Diligence Meeting

The preliminary studies, investigations, research, meetings and compilation of information about a corporation and a proposed new issue that go on during an underwriting are collectively known as *due diligence*. The underwriter, primarily through the syndicate manager, is expected to exercise due diligence (reasonable effort and care) in obtaining all of the information it needs and in verifying its accuracy.

Underwriters are required to conduct a formal due diligence meeting for the benefit of brokers who want information about the issue, the issuer's financial background and the intended use of the proceeds. For issues that are expected to attract national interest, several meetings might be scheduled at different locations around the country. Representatives of the issuer and the underwriter attend these meetings and provide answers to questions from brokers, securities analysts and top institutional accounts.

Blue-Skying the Issue

While the underwriter is putting together the information necessary to bring a new issue to market, it is also engaged in *blue-skying* the security. The syndicate manager takes the preliminary registration packet to the various states in which it plans to offer the securities. Each state has its own registration requirements, and each state wants to be supplied with certain information. If the issue meets the registration requirements of that state, then the issue is blue-skyed and brokers within that state can sell the security to residents of that state.

Most states will exempt securities from individual registration if they meet one or more other requirements—typically listing on a regional or national stock exchange, or qualifying as a NASDAQ or an NMS stock.

Public Offerings vs. Private Placements

Corporate securities can reach the hands of investors through either public offerings or private placements. In a public offering, securities are distributed (sold) to the investing public at large, frequently using a network of broker-dealers to achieve the broadest distribution to the greatest number of investors.

In a private placement, the services of an agent are used to locate select buyers for an issuer's securities. Typically, the transaction size per buyer is quite large in the private placement market, and the buyers tend to be institutional accounts rather than individual retail customers. But private placements may also involve sales to small groups of individuals—especially in conjunction with the distribution of limited partnership program securities and certain commodity pool offerings.

☐ THE UNDERWRITING PROCESS

The first successful securities underwriting in the United States is attributed to Jay Cooke. During the Civil War, he and his force of bond salesmen placed more than $2 billion in U.S. government bonds with private investors throughout the North. By fostering these financial ties between government and investors, Cooke's sales force reinforced the loyalty and patriotism of many investors.

After the war, securities underwriting continued to be critical to the economic development of the United States. Today, publicly owned and financed corporations dominate U.S. business. A business or branch of government that plans to issue securities usually works with an **investment banker,** a securities broker-dealer that specializes in underwriting new issues, bringing securities to market and selling them to investors. Each year, the underwriting activities of investment bankers provide billions of dollars in new equity and debt financing.

An investment banker's functions may include:

- advising corporations on the best ways to raise long-term capital
- raising capital for issuers by distributing new securities
- buying securities from an issuer and reselling them to the public
- distributing large blocks of stock to the public and to institutions

Competitive and Negotiated Underwritings

Competitive bids. An issuer may announce a planned offering of new securities and ask underwriters to bid on the right to distribute the new issue. The underwriter that submits the bid most beneficial to the issuer is awarded the right to underwrite the issue. This is called a *competitive bid.*

Negotiated underwritings. Instead of asking for competitive bids, an issuer may choose an underwriter and negotiate the terms of the offering with that firm. The terms negotiated include the price the issuer receives for the stocks or bonds, the public offering price and, in a bond underwriting, the coupon rate.

Underwriting agreement. After agreement on the terms of the offering, the managing underwriter and the issuer sign an underwriting agreement, which sets forth the terms of the offering and the obligations of the underwriter and the issuer.

Formation of the Underwriting Syndicate

Many new issues are so large that one underwriter cannot handle the entire offering amount on a firm commitment basis. One investment banker, therefore, invites others to form an underwriting syndicate to help defray the underwriting risk and carry out the distribution jointly.

The managing underwriter. The investment banking firm that handles the negotiations with the issuer is known as the *managing underwriter, lead manager* or *manager of the syndicate.* The managing underwriter directs the entire underwriting process, including signing the underwriting agreement with the issuer and directing the due diligence process and the overall marketing and placement of the deal. There may be more than one manager in a syndicate (acting as comanagers) but there can be only one managing underwriter.

The syndicate. The members of the underwriting syndicate make a commitment to the manager to help bring the securities to the public. In a firm commitment offering, all members of the syndicate make a commitment to distribute an agreed upon amount of the issue (their participation or "bracket").

Syndicate members sign a syndicate agreement (the agreement among underwriters or syndicate letter) that describes the responsibilities of the members and manager and allocates syndicate profits. The manager drafts the agreement.

The selling group. Although the members of an underwriting syndicate agree to underwrite an entire offering, they frequently need other firms to help distribute (sell) the securities. The managing underwriter will then invite other broker-dealers to be members of the selling group. Selling group members act as agents with no commitment to the issuer or the selling holders to buy securities.

Distribution of the proceeds. Figure 13 shows how the proceeds of a typical underwriting are distributed.

Freeriding and Withholding

With hot issues (those new issues that have the potential to rise in price quickly), an underwriter could be tempted to make a profit by withholding all or part of the issue from the public and selling after the price has gone up. This practice, called *freeriding and withholding,* violates the NASD Rules of Fair Practice. According to the NASD rules, if public demand exists for the issue, no securities broker-dealer may withhold securities for itself, its employees, its employees' families or its partners.

☐ LEVERAGED BUYOUTS

The 1980s saw a dramatic change in U.S. capital markets. In some instances, small, virtually unknown corporations began taking over major U.S. corporate institutions. Much of this takeover activity was based on the use of the leveraged buyout.

A leveraged buyout (LBO) occurs when one company borrows money to take over another company and pledges the assets of the company it is acquiring to cover the loan. Takeovers of this nature are

FIGURE 13   Who Gets What in an Underwriting

New Issue Incorporated
7% Debenture
$100,000,000
Price 100%

$100,000,000 gross from the sale of the issue to the public.

$99,350,000 of the proceeds goes to the issuer.

New Issue Incorporated
7% Debenture
$100,000,000
Price 100%

$650,000 of the proceeds goes to the underwriters. This fee is known as the gross spread.

$400,000 selling concession paid to syndicate members and selling group members based on the number of bonds sold by each firm.

$130,000 management fee paid to the managing underwriter.

$120,000 underwriting fee paid to all syndicate members based on their pro rata underwriting participation.

almost always very highly leveraged—that is, the acquiring company has put up relatively little of its own money and has borrowed the rest.

The leveraged buyout became very popular in the early 1980s. In 1981, only $3 billion in leveraged buyout business was done in the United States. By 1984, that number had grown to $19 billion, and by 1989 it had reached $62 billion. Many of the leveraged buyouts of this decade were funded through the issuance of what came to be known as *junk bonds*—that is, high-yield bonds with low or no ratings.

The leverage in these buyouts is often so great that even a small change in the profitability of the business could affect the company's ability to meet the terms of the bonds used to fund the buyout. Because of this, junk bonds are subject to wide price swings. In the latter part of the 1980s, many companies that issued junk bonds suffered major losses as the economy slowed and corporate profits fell.

Prior to the beginning of the takeover binge in the 1980s, the LBO was used primarily by employees to buy out all or part of their companies. LBOs allowed people with limited resources to recapitalize a corporation that otherwise may have had to go out of business. After the buyout, the employees would run the business as owners. They had a strong incentive to repay the financing and make the company profitable because failure to do so would mean loss of their livelihoods.

The leveraged buyout as practiced by the corporate raiders of the 1980s was different. Instead of creating capital to restructure businesses in trouble, LBOs often were used to acquire healthy businesses with sound assets. The new owners would then replace the companies' strong asset positions with large debt positions. Profitable divisions were often sold off, and the treasuries of the acquired companies were used by the raiders for other purposes.

The role of the investment banker in the leveraged buyout is usually more than that of underwriter. The acquiring corporation may well have an investment banker active in negotiating the acquisition, as well as in underwriting the securities that finance the deal. The takeover target will usually have an investment banker review the details of the offer. The investment bankers act primarily as intermediaries in these situations, working to get the deal done in the most efficient manner.

The investment banker in mergers and acquisitions. Early in the 1990s, a reversal of the LBO process of the 1980s occurred. Many companies with highly leveraged balance sheets (that is, companies whose capitalization was largely debt) sought to recapitalize and replace the debt with equity investments. The investment adviser served a prominent role in this restructuring, offering advice to the company on the best methods to replace the leverage and bring the company back to an even keel.

In many cases, when a company wants to acquire another company through a merger or an acquisition, the acquiring company will first want to buy a stock position (preferably from some other stockholder with a large position). The acquiring company would then make its offer public. In this case, the investment banker would coordinate the process and manage the details of the acquiring company's bid. The investment banker may even suggest an acquisition to a customer if it knew that the customer was looking to invest or add to its business.

☐ SUMMARY

This chapter introduced the market for newly issued securities, the process of registering a new securities offering, the role an investment banker plays in various types of offerings and the formation and functioning of an underwriting syndicate. The difference between primary and secondary offerings, public offerings and private placements and between competitive and negotiated bidding are important to an understanding of how the industry operates.

We have now seen how securities are issued and how they are traded. The next chapter will review brokerage office procedures and customer accounts, including the critical tasks of keeping track of the firm's and its customers' trading and its investment banking activities.

☐ REVIEW

Check how well you have learned the information contained in this chapter by completing the following sentences.

Every public offering of corporate securities must be made in accordance with the provisions of the

_____

(See page 123)

New issues of securities are also known as

_____

(See page 123)

The needs of corporate business for long-term capital is served by

_____

(See page 124)

The preliminary studies, research and meetings about a proposed new issue are known as

_____

(See page 126)

A planned offering of new securities that requests bids from underwriters is most likely to be

_____

(See page 128)

If an issuer chooses an underwriter to work with it on a new issue rather than requesting bids, the underwriting is most likely to be

_____

(See page 128)

Withholding all or part of a new issue from the public is an illegal practice known as

_____

(See page 129)

When one company borrows money to take over another company and pledges the second company's assets against the loan, the first company is probably engaged in

_____

(See page 129)

Chapter 8

Brokerage Office Procedures and Customer Accounts

"Anyone who thinks the customer isn't important should try doing without him for a period of ninety days."

Anon

Overview

The business of trading securities is not without its share of paperwork. Today, much of the paperwork handled by the operations departments of brokerage firms is posted electronically by carefully designed computer programs. For simplicity, this chapter will follow the paper trail of a customer order. Handling this paper flow accurately is critical to the profitability and ongoing existence of every brokerage firm. Registered representatives (also known as *account executives, financial consultants* and *investment consultants)* and their assistants are responsible for providing accurate and thorough information for opening customer accounts and processing transactions. Firms' operations departments (back offices) are responsible for seeing that transactions occur as directed and reporting the results to the registered representatives and customers.

Some of the trade and account handling procedures each broker-dealer follows are peculiar to the individual firm, while other procedures are required of all firms by securities industry regulators such as the NASD, NYSE and SEC.

□ FUNCTION OF THE OPERATIONS DEPARTMENT

Brokerage firms structure their back office operations in different ways, depending on the mix of investment products offered and whether the firm is a clearing member or an introducing broker. A **clearing member** clears (settles) its own trades, holds customer cash and securities, bills trades, maintains customer ledger accounts and provides a full complement of back office support services. In the language of the SEC, clearing members are usually referred to as *general securities firms* (although not all general securities firms are clearing members).

An **introducing broker** is basically a marketing organization, with few back office operations. Also known as a *fully disclosed broker*, an introducing broker contracts with a clearing member to handle back office work, including customer confirmation billing and ledger account posting—which means that the introducing broker's customers are "fully disclosed," or fully known to the clearing firm.

In contrast to the introducing broker that discloses the names of customers to a clearing firm, there are **omnibus** relationships whereby all trades are executed for, billed to, and settled through a master account (an omnibus account) maintained in the name of the broker-dealer.

What follows is a review of a typical clearing firm's operations, starting with the order department (wire room) and ending with the controller's department.

Order Department (Wire Room)

The order department, which in today's automated environment may be an electronic switch, is a routing center for customer orders entered by the registered representatives. Its function is to get these orders transmitted to an appropriate execution point—either to one of the exchanges or to the OTC trading desk. Once an order is filled or completed, the execution price is reported back to the order department (typically within minutes) and relayed to the registered representative who originated it. Order department personnel check the accuracy and completeness of the execution instructions, account numbers and other order-entry requirements of the NASD and the NYSE. Today, computers often perform this order matching process.

Purchases and Sales Department

The purchases and sales (P&S) department handles customer trade confirmations, trade comparisons on broker-to-broker transactions, settlement date accuracy, customer disclosure requirements on certain transactions, and calculation of accrued interest on bond transactions.

Dividend and Interest Department

The dividend and interest department functions primarily as a collection and redistribution center for distributions that flow into the brokerage house on customer stocks and bonds held *in street name* (owned by the stockholder or bondholder but registered in the name of the broker-dealer or a nominee). In addition to cash dividends, the department handles interest payments on registered bonds, stock dividends, redemptions, stock splits, rights offerings and any special distributions that a corporation or other entity might elect to distribute to its stockholders or bondholders. Further, at some firms the dividend and interest department is also responsible for proxy solicitations, mergers and tender offers.

Cashiering Department

The cashiering department is where transactions are settled—where cash and securities change hands on customer trades and broker-to-broker transactions. This department is responsible for receiving and delivering securities and the applicable monies. It issues payment only if instructed to do so by the margin department. It sends certificates to transfer agents to be transferred into firm or customer name; cashiers will forward the certificates to the customers upon request.

In many firms, the cashiering department is referred to as the *cage*, a reference to the times when the department was secured against robbery and theft by a thickly barred barrier between it and the public.

When a customer sells securities registered in his name, the cashiering department makes certain that the certificates are correctly endorsed and fully negotiable.

Most brokerage firms use a clearing corporation for such services as the delivery of securities and settlement of trades. A clearing corporation can simplify this process by providing specialized comparison clearance and settlement services. A clearing corporation, in effect, acts as a secretary-bookkeeper for a large number of broker-dealer firms. Its function is similar to the role that the Federal Reserve Board plays for its member banks. A clearing corporation totals all trades done on a daily basis for each of its participating firms and balances the books of one firm against those of another. The two entities that handle these functions are the National Securities Clearing Corporation (NSCC) for clearance and the Deposit Trust Corporation (DTC) for settlement.

Margin Department

The margin department interfaces between the registered representatives and the other operations departments. It is also called the *credit department* because it has a significant responsibility for the collection of monies to pay for customer purchases and for monitoring the extension of credit to customers who purchase securities on margin.

A margin account is a collateralized loan account in which a customer expands her trading capital with money borrowed from the brokerage firm in the hopes of earning leveraged profits. In all cases, the stocks or other securities purchased in a margin account are held by the brokerage firm in street name as collateral for the outstanding loan.

From the broker-dealer's viewpoint, margin accounts are good business for two reasons: first, margin account loans generate interest income for the firm; second, with borrowed capital added to the customers' own capital, margin customers typically trade bigger positions, resulting in increased commission revenue.

But there is downside risk. Lending money to customers can lead to losses for the brokerage firm—in the same way as any lending institution suffers if a loan turns bad. The primary risk in a margin account is that the securities securing the loan might decline in value to the point where the loan (the customer **debit balance**) is no longer fully collateralized. Of course, it is true that the customer is legally responsible for repayment of the loan in full (regardless of what happens to the market value of the securities), but some people either cannot or do not pay their obligations.

Current Requirements

Depending on the security, margin requirements as set by the FRB under Regulation T (Reg T) are currently 50%. At 50% margin, for every $100 worth of securities purchased, the customer must deposit $50 and the broker-dealer advances the other $50 as a loan against the securities. If the margin requirement were 90% (which it has been in the past), the customer would deposit $90 and the broker would lend $10. If the margin requirement were 10% (as it was in the 1920s), for $10 a customer could control securities valued at $100—but also have a high degree of risk for the leverage.

New Accounts Department

The new accounts department is responsible for collecting and maintaining records and documentation on each customer account from the time the account is opened. The documentation requirements depend on the answers to the following questions:

- Who is the customer, and is a brokerage account appropriate to this person's situation?
- If this is a joint account, how many people are involved, what legal relationship exists between these people, and who among them will make commitments and decisions?
- If this is a business account, what is the legal entity that represents the organization, and who will make commitments on behalf of the organization?
- If this is a fiduciary account, by what authority is the fiduciary empowered to act?
- Will the account conduct securities business on a cash account basis or in a margin account?

Other Departments

Other departments that are involved in client transactions include the following.

- **Reorganization department.** This department handles any transaction that represents a change in the nature of the securities. This includes such actions as exchanging or transmitting any securities held for clients involved in tender offers, bond calls, redemptions of preferred stock, mergers and acquisitions.
- **Proxy department.** This department is responsible for sending proxy statements to clients whose securities are held in the firm's name. It also sends out financial reports and other publications received from the issuer for its stockholders.
- **Stock record department.** This department maintains the ledger that lists the owners of stock and the location of certificates.
- **Controller's department.** This department is responsible for accounts payable, employee payroll and financial reports to regulatory agencies.

☐ ENTERING A TRADE

To enter a trade for a client, most registered representatives fill out an order ticket and send it to the order (wire) room. The order room is responsible for transmitting the order to the proper market for execution, either directly or through the computer.

Report of Execution

After the execution of a trade, the registered representative receives a report of execution, which must be checked against the order ticket to make sure that everything was done as the client requested. If everything appears to be in order, the execution is reported to the client. If there is any error that appears to be due to either an incorrect ticket or a mistaken execution, the error should be reported immediately to a supervisor or manager. A registered representative should never try to correct an error by making additional trades without approval from a principal of the firm.

Route of a Typical Order

When a client places an order, typically it takes the following route:

1. Client places order with registered representative.
2. Registered representative writes order ticket.
3. Order department receives ticket and transmits order to proper market or exchange for execution, directly or via computer.
4. Market or exchange receives order. If order is executed, it is reported back to the firm's order department.
5. P&S department computes and records the transaction and handles billing and confirmation.
6. Margin department computes the amount the client is required to deposit and transmits this information to the client.
7. Cashiering department receives and delivers securities and money. It issues payments as instructed by the margin department.

Figure 14 illustrates in more detail the route that a typical order takes.

Checking the Confirmation

A confirmation is a printed document that confirms the trade, settlement date, price of the security and amount of money due from or owed to the client. For each transaction, the client must be sent or given a printed confirmation of the trade at or before the completion of the transaction (known as the **settlement date**, which is typically five business days after the transaction date). The registered representative receives a copy of the client's confirmation and checks its accuracy against the order ticket.

Providing Customer Account Statements

Firms are required to send each customer who has a securities position (or whose account has seen any activity) a quarterly statement showing positions and entries in that account. Most firms mail statements

FIGURE 14   Route of a Typical Order

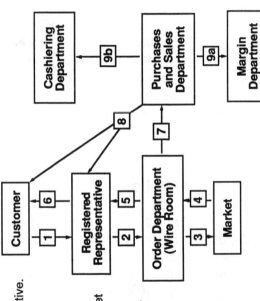

1. Customer places order with registered representative.

2. Registered representative sends order to order department (wire room).

3. Order department sends order to appropriate market for execution.

4. Market sends wire report of execution back to order department.

5. Order department sends report of execution to registered representative.

6. Registered representative calls customer to report execution of order.

7. Order department sends report of trade to P&S department.

8. P&S department sends confirmation to customer and a copy to registered representative.

9. P&S department processes trade for settlement through the:

   a. Margin department, customer credit area;

   b. Cashiering department, which delivers or receives securities from buyer or seller and exchanges monies.

monthly to customers with active accounts (accounts in which there was an entry or a trade) or quarterly to customers with inactive accounts.

☐ CUSTOMER ACCOUNTS

A registered representative may handle many types of accounts. Generally, accounts are classified by three features: ownership (and right to trade), how the securities are paid for and the types of securities bought and sold.

Classification of Accounts

Account ownership. Procedures and relevant regulations vary according to the type of person, group or business that owns the account. The principal types of ownership are:

- individual
- joint (for example, a husband and wife or two business associates)
- partnership
- corporate

Trading authorization. The primary types of trading authorization are:

- **Discretionary.** The registered representative receives written authority from the customer to enter trades without having to consult the customer before each trade.
- **Fiduciary.** The individual given fiduciary responsibility enters the trades for the account.
- **Custodial.** The custodian for the beneficial owner enters all trades.

Payment method. Clients may pay for securities in one of two ways: cash (check) only or cash plus borrowing a portion from the broker-dealer. In cash accounts, clients must pay the full purchase price of the securities. In margin accounts, clients may borrow part of the purchase price from the broker-dealer.

Securities traded. Customers must have special approval to enter into certain types of transactions in their accounts, including trading on margin, short sales, purchases of some limited partnerships and futures trading. Special suitability and experience requirements also exist for options accounts.

Types of Accounts

Joint Accounts

In a joint account, two or more individuals are co-tenants or co-owners of the account. In addition to the appropriate new account form, a joint account agreement must be signed, and the account must be designated as either joint tenants in common (JTIC) or joint tenants with right of survivorship (JTWROS).

Both types of joint account agreements provide that any or all tenants may transact business in the account.

Joint tenants in common. JTIC ownership provides that a deceased tenant's fractional interest in the account is retained by that tenant's estate and is not passed to any surviving tenant(s).

Joint tenants with right of survivorship. JTWROS ownership stipulates that a deceased tenant's interest in the account passes to any surviving tenant(s).

Partnership Accounts

A partnership is an unincorporated association of two or more individuals. In addition to filling out the new account form, the partnership is required to provide a partnership agreement stating which of the partners can make transactions for the account.

Corporate Accounts

When opening an account for a corporation, the registered representative must have a corporate representative complete a new account form. The registered representative must also ascertain which members of the corporation may trade in the account by having the corporation submit a corporate agreement for a cash account. The agreement, signed by the secretary of the corporation and with the corporate seal affixed, identifies the officers authorized to make transactions.

Fiduciary Accounts

A fiduciary is any person legally appointed and authorized to represent another person and act in that person's behalf.

When securities are placed in a fiduciary account, someone other than the owner (the person whose name is on the account) initiates trades. Perhaps the most familiar example of a fiduciary account is a trust account. Money or securities are placed in trust for one person, often a minor, but someone else manages the account. The manager (or trustee) is a fiduciary.

Uniform Gifts to Minors Act Accounts

In Uniform Gifts to Minors Act (UGMA) accounts and Uniform Transfers to Minors Act (UTMA) accounts, an adult (or a bank trust department) must act as custodian for a minor (the beneficial owner). Any kind of security—cash, life insurance, annuity contracts and other forms of property—may be given, and there is no limitation on the dollar amount of the gift. The custodian may be either the donor or a person appointed by the donor, but not necessarily a family member. A gift to a minor under UGMA or UTMA is *irrevocable:* the donor may not take back the gift, nor may the minor return the gift until she has reached the age of majority or the age that the laws of her state have set as the age when the custodianship will terminate (which varies from state to state). When the beneficiary reaches the specified age, the property in the account is transferred into her individual name.

Discretionary Accounts

If an account owner wants to give the registered representative authority to decide the particular security (by name or description), whether to buy or sell or the dollar amount of the security transaction, the client must first sign a trading authorization to make that account a discretionary account. Once trading authorization (sometimes known as *power of attorney*) has been given, the client is legally bound to accept the registered representative's decisions. Discretionary accounts must have prior approval in writing from the broker-dealer or a registered principal representing the broker-dealer.

There are two types of discretionary authority: full discretion, which allows the registered representative to buy and sell securities and also to disburse funds and securities; and the more common limited discretion, which allows the registered representative only to buy and sell securities without conferring with the account owner.

Individual Retirement Accounts

Individual retirement accounts (IRAs) were created by Congress in 1974 as a way of encouraging people to save towards their retirements.

The Economic Recovery Tax Act of 1981 (ERTA) allowed all IRA participants to fully deduct the amount contributed to their IRAs from their taxable income. The Tax Reform Act of 1986 (TRA 1986) changed the deductibility limits, lowering them for individuals who are covered by other qualified plans. If an individual is not actively participating in other qualified plans, however, the full amount of the contribution to the IRA is still deductible.

Taxpayers are free to appoint an IRA custodian of their choice, selecting from a range of financial service vendors, securities broker-dealers, banks and savings institutions, insurance carriers, credit unions and mutual fund distributors.

Keogh (HR-10) Plans

For anyone who is self-employed or owns a small business or professional practice, a Keogh plan offers similar tax advantages and retirement coverage as are found with corporate retirement programs.

Keogh plans are intended for self-employed individuals and owner-employees of nonincorporated business concerns or professional practices.

Included in the self-employed category are independent contractors, consultants, freelancers and anyone else who files and pays self-employment social security taxes. Also included are part-timers who work full time somewhere else.

The term "owner-employee" refers to sole proprietors who rely on their businesses for their livelihood. The term also applies to partnership establishments in which each partner works for the partnership as an employee and also owns a stake in the business.

Annuity Plans

An annuity is a contract between an individual and an insurance company, usually purchased for retirement income. Investors, called *annuitants*, contribute money to an annuity plan either in a lump sum or as periodic contractual payments. At some future time (specified in the contract), the owner of the annuity plan will begin receiving regular income distributions.

Tax-deferred annuities (TDAs)—sometimes called *tax-sheltered annuities (TSAs)*—are designed for long-term savings only. To ensure this objective, TDAs (like IRAs and other retirement plans) are subject to tax penalties if the savings are withdrawn before the participant retires.

Investment Objectives and Suitability

Every customer has unique financial objectives and goals. It is important that enough information is gathered about a customer to enable investment recommendations to reflect these objectives and goals accurately. The first transaction should be entered only after the preliminary information gathering has been accomplished and an investment suggestion has been accepted by the customer.

Some of the basic financial objectives of customers follow.

Preservation of capital. For many people, their single most important investment objective is to preserve the capital they have worked so hard to accumulate. A person with this as the most important objective would not be willing to invest in many speculative or volatile securities. In general, when clients speak of "safety," they mean preservation of capital from losses due to credit or financial risk. **Financial risk** is the danger of losing all or part of the principal amount invested.

Current income. Many investors, particularly retirees and others on fixed incomes, want to generate additional current income from their investments. Corporate bonds, municipal bonds, government and agency securities, income-oriented mutual funds, some stocks (for example, utilities and real estate investment trusts), money-market funds, annuities and some direct participation programs (DPPs) are among the investments that can contribute current income through dividend or interest payments.

Capital growth. "Growth" refers to an increase in the value of an investment over time. This growth can come from increases in the value of the security, the reinvestment of dividends and interest, or both. Investors seek growth in order to meet a variety of needs (retirement planning, funding a child's education, travel or a vacation home, to name a few). The most common growth-oriented investments are common stock and stock mutual funds.

Tax advantages. Many clients seek ways to reduce their taxes. Some products, such as IRAs and annuities, allow interest to accumulate tax deferred (no taxes are paid until the investor withdraws money from the account). Other products, such as many municipal bonds, offer tax-free interest income.

Portfolio diversification. An investor may have reasons based on other than personal or financial factors for choosing an investment. Investment professionals frequently encounter investors whose portfolios are concentrated in only one or a few securities or investments. Because such concentrations of investments expose these customers to much higher risks, portfolio diversification becomes an important objective. Typical of these customers are retirees with large profit-sharing distributions of one company's stock. Portfolios can be diversified using a number of elements, including:

- type of issue (equity, debt, packaged and so on)
- geography
- maturity
- purpose of issue
- security
- quality

Liquidity. Some people want immediate access to their money at all times. A product is liquid if the customer can sell it quickly at face amount (or very close to it) or at a fair market price without losing significant principal. Stock, for example, has varying degrees of liquidity (depending on many factors, including safety, number of shares outstanding and the market's perception of the issuer), while DPPs, annuities and bank CDs are generally considered illiquid. Real estate is the classic example of an illiquid product because of the time and money it takes to convert it into cash.

Speculation. Among the investment objectives a customer might have is the need to speculate—that is, to seek higher than average returns in exchange for higher than average risks. Speculation is a legitimate investment objective.

□ SUMMARY

In order for a broker-dealer to be competitive and succeed as a firm, the strength and effectiveness of its back office (operations department) is most important.

The next chapter introduces the topics of economics and analysis and their use by (and effects on) the securities industry.

□ REVIEW

Check how well you have learned the information contained in this chapter by completing the following sentences.

A broker-dealer that settles its own trades, holds customer cash and securities and maintains customer accounts is known as

_____

(See page 136)

A broker-dealer that contracts with a clearing firm to handle its customer accounts, billing, cash and securities is known as

_____

(See page 136)

The department that handles the transmission of orders to an exchange or to the OTC trading desk is the

_____

(See page 136)

The department that handles customer trade confirmations, settlement date accuracy and accrued bond interest calculations is the

_____

(See page 137)

The collection and redistribution center for cash and stock dividends is the

_____

(See page 137)

Transactions are settled and cash and securities are handled by the

_____

(See page 137)

Calculation of customers' credit and debit balances and Reg T requirements is handled by the

_____

(See page 138)

The department that is responsible for collecting and maintaining customer records is the

_____

(See page 139)

The printed document that contains all of the information about a trade that is sent to the customer at or before settlement date is the

_____

(See page 141)

The three primary types of trading authorization are

_____

(See page 143)

Chapter 9

Economics, Analysis and the Securities Industry

"An economist's guess is liable to be as good as anybody else's."

Will Rogers

Overview

The securities industry and the economic environment are part of the same whole. Stock markets, bond markets, money markets and all other markets react to and cause a reaction in the economic environment. Just like the natural environment, a ripple in one part of the pond causes a ripple in another part of the pond. In the world of money, it is sometimes hard to tell when the economy is moving the markets or when the markets are moving the economy.

Take, for example, the Great Depression. Some people feel that the lean years of the 1930s were brought on by the stock market crash of 1929. Many economists tell us, however, that the depression was in fact an economic reaction to restrictive monetary and fiscal (tax) policy combined with global protectionism and reduced international trading; in their view, the market crash anticipated the negative effects of these factors on the economy. Still, there is no doubt that the crash affected the economy dramatically, especially with the subsequent failures in the banking system.

☐ ECONOMIC AND BUSINESS CYCLES

Economics and economic activity are studied by those who want to determine the overall health and vitality of a country's economy. In particular, economists employed within the securities industry try to measure and predict how the economy's ups and downs will affect investment instruments and corporations in a variety of industries.

Few measurable factors have greater influence on the securities markets than the economy. Business cycles, changes in the money supply, actions of the Federal Reserve Board and a host of complex international monetary factors affect securities prices and trading.

Business Cycles

Throughout the United States' history, periods of economic expansion have followed periods of economic contraction in a long-term pattern called the *business cycle*. Long-term business cycles go through four phases:

1. expansion
2. peak
3. contraction
4. trough

Figure 15 illustrates the cyclical nature of this pattern of expansion and contraction.

Expansion, also known as *recovery*, is characterized by increases in business activity throughout the economy. When the **peak** of this activity increase is reached, economists call that state *prosperity*. As business activity begins an overall period of decline, the economy is said to be going through a **contraction**. To an economist, mild short-term contractions that last two to six consecutive quarters (6 to 18 months) are known as *recessions*. More severe contractions of longer duration may be deemed *depressions*. At the bottom of a contraction is a period in which business activity stops its decline and begins the long road back through expansion to prosperity. This bottom of the business cycle is known as a **trough**.

FIGURE 15   The Business Cycle

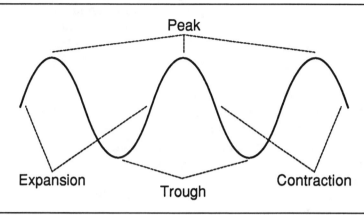

The U.S. Commerce Department defines a depression somewhat more strictly than most economists do, primarily for political reasons. According to the U.S. Commerce Department, the economy is in a recession when a decline in real output of goods and services (the gross national product) lasts for six months (two quarters) or more. It defines a depression as a very severe downturn lasting for several years with unemployment rates greater than 15%.

Although periods of prosperity always follow hard times and hard times again yield to prosperity, knowing when the economy is on an upward or a downward slope is not always a simple matter. In the normal course of events, some industries or corporations will prosper as others face problems. A long-term downward slope will be interrupted by temporary upturns that may or may not signal a return to prosperity, and vice versa. Economists take into account many factors when trying to determine where the economy is in the business cycle.

Gross National Product

The annual economic output of a nation (all of the goods and services produced by the people, businesses and government units within it) is known as its *gross national product (GNP)*. The United States' GNP includes personal consumption, government purchases (federal payrolls, defense spending, office supplies, etc.), gross private investment (including new buildings, machinery and inventories), foreign investments in the United States and the total value of exports. In periods of recession, the GNP decreases. During periods of expansion, the GNP increases.

When comparing the GNP of one period with the GNP of another, a person must take into account changes in the relative prices of products that have occurred during the intervening time. Economists adjust GNP figures to *constant dollars*, rather than attempt to compare actual dollars. This allows economists and others who use GNP figures to compare the actual purchasing power of the dollars, rather than the dollars themselves. Otherwise, it would be nearly impossible to compare the GNP of recessionary periods (like the 1930s) with that of inflationary periods (like the 1970s).

In the early 1990s, government economists began measuring activity as gross domestic product (GDP). GDP differs from GNP in that the value of goods and services produced abroad by U.S. companies is excluded from GDP.

Price Levels

Inflation. Inflation is a persistent and measurable rise in the general level of prices and is generally associated with periods of expansion and high levels of employment. Inflation itself is not bad, and mild inflation actually encourages economic growth. Gradually increasing prices tend to stimulate business investments, both domestic and foreign, and help maintain full employment and a growing GNP. It is when inflation reaches unacceptably high levels that it is considered detrimental to the economy. High inflation can cause hardships for many, particularly those on fixed incomes.

Deflation. Deflation is a persistent and measurable fall in the general level of prices. During periods of deflation, the production of goods and services exceeds the demand for them. Deflation is rare and usually occurs during severe economic downturns when unemployment is on the rise.

Stagflation. Stagflation is a relatively new term in economic circles and is used to describe those periods of high unemployment (stagnation) coupled with rising prices (inflation). The major problems experienced during periods of economic stagflation are that any effort made to increase employment will also increase inflation and any action taken to decrease inflation will probably also decrease employment.

Consumer Price Index. All prices do not change at the same rate. Some rise or fall more rapidly than others. The most prominent measure of price changes in general is the Consumer Price Index (CPI). The CPI measures the rate of increase or decrease in consumer prices for such things as food, housing, transportation, medical care, clothing, electricity, entertainment and services. The CPI is put out monthly by the U.S. Bureau of Labor Statistics and represents a composite of selected consumer items in selected cities over a one-month period.

Economic Indicators

According to economic analysts, the U.S. economy rides a continuous roller coaster (the business cycle) characterized by periods of expansion and increasing affluence alternating with periods of recession, during which business activity contracts and unemployment increases. In an attempt to improve the understanding of where the U.S. economy is and where it is going in the business cycle, analysts have identified certain measurable factors within the economy that appear to be linked to the business cycle. They refer to these economic factors as *indicators*. Economists believe that tracking measurable movements in these indicators can give analysts a better idea as to how the economy is currently faring and can also help analysts and others who use these indicators to predict its future direction.

□ GOVERNMENT ECONOMIC POLICY

The government can affect the country's economic system through one of its two economic policies: fiscal policy or monetary policy. The president's and the federal government's policies on taxation and spending make up the country's **fiscal policy**. The government attempts to influence the country's economic health through its powers to tax and spend. The government will make decisions based on its fiscal policy that will have both direct and indirect impacts on aggregate supply and demand.

The FRB's policies on the size, movement and growth of the money supply compose its **monetary policy**. The FRB works through its influence on the banking system, the money supply, bank lending and interest rates. The actions the FRB can take to increase or decrease the money supply are part of its monetary policy.

Money and Banking

A significant factor in the health and growth of the economy is the money supply—the amount of money available for consumers and businesses to spend. Commercial banks (as opposed to savings and loans) deal in **demand deposits**. A demand deposit is money left with a bank (or borrowed from a bank and left on deposit) that the depositing customer has the right to withdraw on demand. A **time deposit**, in contrast, is a deposit of money that the depositing customer has agreed not to withdraw for a specified period of time or without sufficient advance notice to the depository bank, should the deposit institution elect to enforce the time or notice requirement.

Definition of Money

Although to most people the term "money" means the bills and coins in their wallets and pockets, in the world of economics, it means more than the cash people carry. To an economist, money includes loans, credit and an assortment of other liquid instruments. Economists divide money into four categories, depending on the type of account in which it is kept.

1. **M1.** The most readily available type of money, M1 consists of currency and demand deposits that can be converted to currency immediately. This is the money consumers use for ordinary purchases of goods and services.
2. **M2.** In addition to M1, M2 includes some time deposits that are fairly easy to convert into demand deposits. These time deposits include savings accounts, money-market funds and overnight repurchase agreements.

3. **M3.** In addition to M1 and M2, M3 includes time deposits of more than $100,000 and repurchase agreements with terms longer than one day.
4. **L.** L includes M1, M2 and M3 plus other long-term liquid assets, including T bills, savings bonds, commercial paper, bankers' acceptances and Eurodollar holdings of U.S. residents.

Most money (M1) is stored in the form of demand deposits; it is checkbook money. M1 is the largest component of the money supply. M2, although smaller in total value, is also of great significance to economists and securities analysts with their eyes on credit markets.

Monetary Policies of the Federal Reserve Board

Monetary policy determines how the FRB acts to influence the money supply and, consequently, the economy. In 1913, Congress established the Federal Reserve System (Fed) to regulate the U.S. banking system and money supply. The Fed consists of twelve regional Federal Reserve Banks, 24 branch banks and hundreds of national and state banks that belong to the system. Under the direction of the FRB (which consists of seven members appointed by the president of the United States), the Fed performs the following functions:

- regulates the U.S. money supply;
- sets reserve requirements for members;
- supervises the printing of currency;
- clears fund transfers throughout the system; and
- examines members to ensure their compliance with federal regulations.

Indirectly, the FRB determines how much money is available for businesses and consumers to spend and is therefore one of the most powerful factors in the U.S. economy.

Fiscal Policy

As the Fed manages the economy through monetary policy, the president and Congress attack economic problems through fiscal policy. The term "fiscal" refers to budgets (as in *fiscal year*), and "fiscal policy" refers to governmental budget decisions, which can include increases or decreases in:

- federal spending
- money raised through taxation
- federal budget deficits or surpluses

Fiscal policy is based on the assumption that by using the tools and policies at its disposal, the government can:

- reduce the rate of inflation by reducing aggregate demand for goods and services if price levels are excessive; or
- increase the rate of inflation by increasing aggregate demand if low inflation or deflation is contributing to unemployment and economic stagnation.

Congress uses fiscal policy just as the Fed uses monetary policy to control the severity of fluctuations in the economy. The condition of the economy prompts government intervention, and government actions, in turn, help shape the economy.

The Stock Market

Monetary policies frequently have considerable influence on the stock market. By raising margin requirements, the Federal Reserve can restrain speculation in stocks. Even more significant, the Fed's ability to control the money supply can influence stock prices. If the Fed increases the money supply, credit is easier to obtain. As credit becomes easier to obtain, interest rates drop, and lower interest rates tend to encourage bullish stock markets.

Similarly, lowering tax rates may stimulate spending by those individuals or businesses that now find themselves with more of their earnings to spend. Like easier credit, reductions in tax rates tend to stimulate stock market investments. Raising taxes, of course, tends to have the opposite effect by reducing the amount of money available for business and consumer spending or for investment.

Interest Rates

The cost of credit (interest rates) depends on supply and demand. In periods of easy money when the credit supply exceeds demand, interest rates fall. Conversely, interest rates tend to rise when the Fed is tightening the money supply and demand exceeds supply. By influencing the money supply, the Federal Reserve affects interest rates.

Business Cycles

The power of the FRB to influence interest rates and expand credit has a direct impact on business. Monetary policy helps determine how much money is available for business investments. The Fed's power is considerable, but not absolute. Not all commercial banks are members of the Fed, and the Fed exerts little influence over international banking. Nevertheless, financial analysts, investors and the general public watch the Fed closely, knowing its policies influence business cycles.

Government spending and taxation (fiscal policy) also influence the shape of the business cycle. Increases in government spending, as politicians are eager to tell voters at election time, tend to be inflationary. Money that the government injects into the economy increases the demand for goods and services, thereby driving up prices. Lower government spending, naturally, has the opposite effect, reducing inflation and lowering employment.

□ INTERNATIONAL MONETARY FACTORS

Balance of Payments

One important link between U.S. and international economies is the money that flows between the United States and other countries. The accounting record that keeps track of all such currency exchanges is called the *balance of payments.*

The balance of payments may run a surplus (more money entering the country than leaving it) or a deficit (more money leaving the country than entering it). A deficit may occur when high interest rates in another country attract savings dollars of U.S. citizens or corporations. Because of this deficit, citizens of other countries accumulate more dollars than they need for their payments to the United States, and there is an excess supply of U.S. dollars abroad.

The largest component of the balance of payments is the **balance of trade**, the export and import of merchandise (not services). On the U.S. credit side are sales of U.S. products to foreign countries; on the debit side are U.S. purchases of foreign goods that cause U.S. dollars to flow out of the country. Until 1970, the U.S. annual trade balance was positive every year during this century: the United States made more money on exports than it spent on imports. Since then, the country has consistently traded at a deficit. A favorable balance of trade means more exports than imports. An unfavorable balance of trade means more imports than exports.

□ TECHNICAL ANALYSIS

Both technical and fundamental market and stock analyses are based on the premise that price movements of the stock market can be predicted. Fundamental analysts are usually interested in the longer term (6 to 18 months) behavior of investments in particular companies or industries. Fundamentalists concentrate on broad-based economic trends, current business conditions within an industry and the quality of the stock of a particular corporation. The technical analyst, on the other hand, is more interested in forecasting short-term trends based on patterns of trading activity, often as revealed on charts. For the technical analyst, the decision to buy or sell depends almost entirely on market activity and market trends.

Many market analysts use both fundamental and technical information and tools in making trading decisions. Often, they rely primarily on fundamental analysis to determine which transactions to make and primarily on technical analysis for timing entries to and exits from the market.

Technical analysts attempt to evaluate the strengths and weaknesses of the market at a specific time. They try to predict bull markets (when investors are optimistic and prices are rising) and bear markets (when investors are pessimistic and prices are falling). In addition, they may examine trading patterns of industry groups and individual stocks in an effort to predict which stocks are likely to go up or down.

☐ FUNDAMENTAL ANALYSIS

Fundamental analysis concentrates on uncovering and analyzing information about an issuer's fiscal health, markets, products and performance. The securities industry employs fundamental analysts to help it select healthy companies in which to invest. To determine the economic soundness of a corporation, fundamental analysts focus on such factors as the economic and political climate, the outlook for particular industries and the competitive position of individual companies. The fundamentalist generally tends to have a long-term outlook.

Industry Analysis

Once they have assessed the state of the economy, fundamental analysts look at particular industries to see which are likely to fare best as the economy proceeds along its upward or downward course. They look for industries that offer better-than-average long-term investment opportunities. Some industries are more affected by business cycles than others. Investors find it useful to distinguish among the four types of industries and investments: defensive, cyclical, growth and special situation.

Corporate Analysis

After considering the state of the economy and the health of various industries, fundamental analysts try to select companies whose stocks offer good investment opportunities. They analyze the position of a company within its industry by looking at such matters as competitive position in the industry, prospects for growth and stability, and current financial position (as evidenced by financial statements).

To ascertain a company's ability to compete in its industry, analysts examine the company's current and probable future market share, whether it is a leader within its industry and whether it is introducing new products that might increase its market share and profitability.

Fundamental analysts are concerned with the growth and stability of a company. They look at the quality of the firm's management and historical earnings trends. They consider how its projected growth compares with that of its competitors and whether its growth is stable or erratic. Analysts also examine a corporation's capitalization and use of working capital. They try to pinpoint stocks that afford the investor maximum potential for growth, stability and profits.

Financial Statements

Fundamental analysts use the financial statements of a corporation to analyze its profitability, financial strength and operating efficiency. The balance sheet can be used to analyze the solvency, liquidity and capital structure of the corporation. Analysts use the relationships between these numbers (such as the ratio of equity to total capitalization) to judge the financial health of the company.

Companies traded on the principal exchanges and NASDAQ are required to submit an annual report to each stockholder. Most listed companies also issue quarterly financial statements that include (among other financial documents) a balance sheet and an income statement. The annual report usually includes other financial reports such as the retained earnings statement and funds statement. The balance sheet and income statement, however, are critical tools for analyzing a company's financial situation.

☐ IMPACT OF THE INDUSTRY ON THE ECONOMY

The securities industry in the United States is a major contributor to the economy. It employs hundreds of thousands of individuals and spends tens of billions of dollars annually on compensation, purchases and other expenses. Even more importantly, it raises huge amounts of capital for business and government and provides liquidity for investments.

The ability to access capital easily is called *liquidity*. Liquidity is an important factor in economic success. Without the ability to move and remove capital freely, people cease to invest. That cessation of investment would have tremendous negative effects on the economy. The securities industry provides that liquidity. It provides well-managed, centralized markets in which all can participate.

To understand the importance of liquidity in the economy, consider the reaction to the crash of 1929 and compare it to that of the crash of 1987. When the market fell in 1929, the amount of money in the economy was dramatically reduced. The Federal Reserve Board failed to act decisively in response, and many banks and broker-dealers failed in the ensuing bank collapse.

On the other hand, when the market crashed in 1987, the Fed injected massive amounts of cash into the system and stimulated liquidity in the market. In addition, the Fed coordinated with other central banks around the world. As all of these institutions reacted in concert, the market stabilized and the damage was contained.

The markets serve other functions as well. They provide the economy with an advance signal. As companies announce earnings and the markets react, governments and business use the reaction to plan and strategize. They also provide investors and borrowers with a venue in which to raise capital to invest. Without this venue, business would be much less able to expand and take advantage of profit opportunities.

The process of capital formation is the ultimate function of the market. Without this ability, most businesses would never get past the sole proprietor stage. Employment would be limited and the economic benefits of expansion, equipment purchases and investment in plant and equipment would be dramatically reduced.

Even those businesses that never raise capital in the stock or bond markets enjoy the economic benefits of these markets. The capital they raise through private sources would be in constant demand elsewhere. This excess demand would drive the cost of capital higher, severely reducing the ability of American business to grow and compete.

The variety of products in the market affects the economy, too. Imagine if businesses could raise capital only by borrowing. Many would severely curtail business expansion. Newer businesses and innovative businesses with uncertain revenues would have no ability to raise capital (because creditors would be unlikely to lend to them). The advent of the futures market has dramatically increased the ability of producers and consumers to plan and budget. And options provide investors with an opportunity to transfer investment risks. All of these products affect the market's viability and, thus, the economy as a whole.

To gauge the impact of the securities industry on the economy, one need only consider its impact on popular culture. Wall Street has created its own mini-industry of books, movies, newspapers, journals and newsletters. It has spawned myths and has reduced mythically powerful figures to ordinariness. It has turned a sleepy little village on an island in New York Harbor into the economic center of the world. And today, all of America watches the markets' fluctuations in the daily news. Wall Street—that is, the nationwide securities industry—reflects what is happening in the country.

□ POLITICAL EVENTS AND THEIR IMPLICATIONS

Politics and political events impact the markets, whether by design, as in fiscal policy, or by accident, as in the assassination of a president.

Elections are highly charged political times. During campaigns, attention is focused on what the candidates say they will do and how they will do it. Investors respond to these campaigns as well as to the election results. If the winning candidate's platform is good for business, investors would most likely buy equities to participate in the business growth. If the winning candidate suggests action that might be bad for business, such as excessive tax increases, many equity investors would most likely sell, driving the market lower.

Consider the effect of a global crisis, such as a war. Aside from the obvious redirection of investment from productive, usable manufacturing to nonproductive military expenditure, there would be other direct economic impacts. The uncertainty of victory would cause investors to reduce their risk exposure. They would likely sell equities and invest in more secure investments. And the lost production from the military theater of conflict would also be likely to reduce the profitability of any companies doing business there. Finally, the costs of the war would eventually have to be paid, and that means increased taxes or deficit spending—both of which would have significant impacts on the markets.

The political events on the world scene impact the U.S. economy, too. A weakening in the Japanese stock market might mean that Japanese investors would reduce their investments abroad to cover domestic losses. They would then repatriate their investment capital homeward. That money would no longer be available in the U.S. markets, and liquidity would be decreased. The result: less money to invest, which means lower demand, which means lower prices for investments.

Even positive events such as the democratization of Eastern Europe can have a mixed effect on the U.S. economy. There would most likely be increased trading opportunities as those countries expand and modernize; however, there would also be a significant demand for capital in that market, driving the price of capital higher. This increased demand would translate into higher interest rates, reduced global liquidity and, possibly, inflation.

In fact, any political event can be recast into its economic impact. The real issue is, to which event is the market going to pay the most heed? The market has a mind of its own. Investments in securities are made thousands of times each day. Each investor action represents one small part of the collective response to change the market demonstrates daily. Only the largest of events can dominate the market, and only for the period immediately surrounding the event. Then, as soon as the event is assimilated into the collective plans and consciousness of investors, the market continues on.

□ SUMMARY

Local, national and global economic events impact the securities industry daily, in both measurable and immeasurable ways. Analyzing how economic events shape the securities markets is an important task for the economists and analysts employed by broker-dealers.

Analysts are also employed within the industry to monitor the investment potential of individual firms. These analysts devote their time and efforts to tracking the profitability of companies and measuring how well they compete in their industries.

Economists, analysts and others are discussed in more detail in the next chapter, "Jobs and Functions in the Securities Industry."

□ REVIEW

Check how well you have learned the information contained in this chapter by completing the following sentences.

The four phases of the business cycle are

_____

(See page 154)

When a decline in real output of goods and services lasts for six months or more, economists term it a

_____

(See page 154)

The annual economic output of a nation is known as its

_____

(See page 155)

Inflation is a persistent and measurable rise in the general level of prices and is generally associated with periods of

_____

(See page 156)

Economists track the economy and attempt to predict its future direction by analyzing

_____

(See page 157)

The taxation and spending policies of the president and the federal government make up the country's

_____

(See page 157)

The Federal Reserve Board's policies on the size, growth and movement of the money supply make up its

(See page 158)

The largest component of the United States' balance of payments is the

(See page 162)

Chapter 10

Jobs and Functions in the Securities Industry

"The job of a professional manager is not to like people. It is not to change people. It is to put their strengths to work."

Peter Drucker

Overview

The business of moving investment capital from those who have it to those who need it demands the talents of hundreds of thousands of people every day of the year. Within the securities industry there are many fascinating career possibilities, including jobs in such areas as sales, marketing, analysis, accounting, research, human resources, administrative support, trading, training and legal services.

Every firm in the industry has its own unique culture and shape—not all firms employ people in every job category. Some of this is due to specialization in certain investments or securities—firms that sell primarily mutual funds will have different staffing needs than firms that specialize in investment banking. Other firms are structured in such a way that certain functions are handled externally. Some broker-dealers employ outside firms to handle clearing, operations, transfer, collections or training.

Following are descriptions of just a few of the hundreds of job opportunities within the securities industry.

□ ADMINISTRATION

Clerical and Operations (Back Office) Staff

In the world of securities, only those in control of their paperwork can be successful. The SEC, the exchanges and the NASD have established very specific recordkeeping requirements for broker-dealers.

This deluge of paper is the responsibility of the operations and clerical support staff (also known as the *back office*). The term "back office" has its roots in the way broker-dealers used to lay out their floor plans. Registered representatives were typically situated at the front of the office so customers would have easy access to them. Cashiers, people handling securities, and those operating the Teletype and order functions were situated at the back of the office.

The operations department is essential to the successful operation of a securities firm. In the late 1960s, the industry experienced greatly increased levels of business and such a severe paper crunch that the NYSE stopped trading each Wednesday to allow firms to catch up on their paperwork. At that time, much posting and recordkeeping was done manually—the sophisticated microfilm methods and computer networks of today did not yet exist. As the industry grew, so did the application of computerized recordkeeping and reporting, enabling broker-dealers to keep up with the demands of the paper and nonpaper transactions they handle each day.

As a result of computerization, jobs were streamlined and new employment opportunities were created. Following are some of the departments and functions common to today's highly sophisticated operations departments.

Collections. Processes Regulation T calls; applies for NYSE margin extensions; collects money due in accounts. (These activities generally take place within the margin department.)

Customer accounts. Maintains existing customer accounts; processes customer requests for distributions of cash and securities; processes firm requests for additional equity from customers.

New accounts. Establishes and updates customer accounts; collects customer information and necessary signatures and forms.

Retirement accounts. Supports and processes the administration of retirement accounts (IRAs, Keoghs, 401Ks, other corporate pension and profit-sharing plans and so on).

Dividends. Pays dividends, stock splits and bond interest in a timely and accurate manner.

Trade control. Supports the purchase and sale of equity securities; monitors the automatic trade-processing systems.

Reorganization. Processes tender offers, redemptions and bond exchanges; notifies the representatives of any options that may be available; processes any changes.

Receive and deliver. Takes in and sends out securities.

Microfilm. Creates and maintains microfilm records of all securities and official documents.

Retail liaison. Addresses customer problems or communications that cannot be handled through normal channels.

Stock transfer. Transfers securities into and out of the firm in a timely and accurate manner.

Mutual funds. Settles inside (proprietary) and outside mutual funds.

Stock loan. Processes stock loans as needed to cover short sales or firm inventory needs.

Administrative services. Supplies mailing and printing support; oversees document filing and creation; administers typing and reception services.

Facilities planning. Maintains physical building and equipment; orders supplies; repairs and maintains furniture and equipment; coordinates telephone equipment and services.

Central document services. Stores documents for future retrieval; maintains records according to SEC, NYSE, MSRB and NASD guidelines.

Computer operations. Enters key customer data into the computer system; operates the computer facilities.

Wire operator. Runs the order entry system.

☐ RESEARCH AND MANAGEMENT

Research Analyst

The securities industry employs research analysts to scrutinize potential investments and suggest actions concerning those investments. Research analysts study corporate financial statements, evaluate industry data, watch general market trends and travel to and investigate potential investment opportunities first hand. Often gathered during visits with key personnel in the companies they are researching, information uncovered by analysts is then passed on to the brokers in the form of buy, hold or sell recommendations. Research analysts tend to specialize in a particular industry, such as chemicals, automotive or hospitality. They track the growth of the industry as well as both established and new companies in that industry. They monitor and report on industry trends that could impact the particular companies they follow. Many broker-dealers also have an economist to track national and world economic events and report on the potential effect national and international economic events will have on industries, companies and investment opportunities.

Research analysts are employed by broker-dealers, banks, mutual fund companies, insurance companies and other large investors. They generally have some form of accounting or finance background, and many have worked in the industry in which they specialize.

Legal and Compliance

The legal and compliance department is the regulatory group within each brokerage firm. This department has the responsibility of ensuring that the actions of all employees, particularly production people, meet regulatory guidelines and firm policies.

The legal needs of a brokerage firm are many. When you realize that every order ticket, retirement plan, account agreement, trust arrangement, underwriting and so on represents a contract, you begin to understand the complexity of a broker-dealer's legal requirements. The legal department is involved in every aspect of the firm's business and is devoted to making sure that the firm can meet the legal requirements of the various securities regulators while still being able to attract business and make a profit.

Compliance departments rely heavily on management reports and computer analysis of account holdings and trading patterns. They review concentrations of securities in an account, excessive trading, irregular issuance of checks and unusually large cash deposits as part of the monitoring process.

Legal and compliance departments are generally staffed by people with backgrounds in law and finance. They have a strong knowledge of (and interest in) the industry regulatory environment. They become involved in such areas as customer complaints, audits of branches and departments, information gathering and investigations by regulatory agencies and approval of advertising and other communications.

Portfolio Management

Many investors lack the time, experience and expertise to manage their own investments. For others, there comes a point when their investment portfolio becomes large enough to require outside professional assistance. In both of these situations, a portfolio manager is often the answer. This individual specializes in managing investments for other people, either on an individual basis or as a portfolio manager for an investment company.

Many firms offer a managed portfolio service for larger accounts, where a portfolio manager will select investments based on a customer's goals and objectives and enter trades as deemed appropriate. For this service, the customer pays either an annual fee or commissions charged on trades, or both. Managed portfolio accounts will often receive reduced commission rates, or the management fee may include brokerage commissions.

Investment company portfolio managers invest on behalf of the shareholders of a mutual fund. Their investment selections depend on the stated objectives of the mutual fund and any investment limitations set up by the fund. The mutual fund managers charge the fund an annual fee for their services, usually less than 1% of the portfolio value.

Both types of portfolio managers function in much the same way. They review the portfolio on a regular basis, assessing the performance of investments and looking for ways to improve on the portfolio's holdings. This includes extensive study and research as well as actively following the markets.

Portfolio management is often a committee affair, with different managers specializing in different securities or industries. This way, the portfolios benefit from the attention of more than one professional manager. Because there are so many potential investments, it would be impossible for any one person to follow them all.

Marketing

The marketing department serves a critical function. It creates, designs and obtains approvals for all of the advertising and sales literature that is circulated by the firm and its employees. In addition, it plans sales strategies, identifies client needs and supports new product development. The people in this department must work closely with the branch and sales system to understand their needs, with senior management to determine how to move towards corporate goals, with administration to coordinate printing and distribution efforts and with compliance to ensure that all regulatory requirements are met. Some firms have a centralized marketing function, but in many firms marketing is subdivided by product group. Mutual funds, retirement planning, portfolio management, investment banking, human resources, fixed income, underwriting, options and others have very specialized needs that are often best met by a dedicated marketing staff. People employed in the marketing departments of broker-dealers come from a wide range of backgrounds, including law, marketing, sales, journalism and liberal arts.

Human Resources

The day-to-day needs of the employees of a broker-dealer are usually met by the human resources department. This department handles hiring; training; employee records; vacation schedules; insurance plans; 401Ks; pension, profit-sharing and retirement plans; performance reviews; promotions; and a host of other responsibilities. An employee's first contact with a broker-dealer is usually with its human resources department.

Recruiting

While branch managers are on the front line in the drive to hire good people, the human resources department of most firms provides extensive support to that effort. That support includes providing advertising aimed to bring in candidates, setting minimum education and experience standards and managing the testing of potential employees. The human resources department also may be involved in coordinating required licensing exams and setting compensation levels for employees.

There is a variety of jobs in the human resources department, ranging from recruitment and selection specialists to support staff who ensure that the department runs smoothly. Their key function is to ensure that their firm's staffing needs are met properly and at a reasonable cost and that employee morale is maintained.

Training

Training in the securities industry varies from firm to firm. Some firms provide little or no training to their personnel, relying on outside resources for exam preparation, sales skills and management seminars. Other firms have extensive training departments that handle almost every aspect of the securities business.

Most firms provide some level of orientation training to new employees through the branch or through the human resources department in the main office. Beyond that, training needs are highly job dependent.

Most of the industry's training dollars are focused on helping registered representatives to do their jobs better. This can include training in telephone marketing skills, product training or other skills to improve production, compensation and customer satisfaction. This training may be provided by internal trainers, but many firms hire outside consultants to design or deliver all or a part of their training.

☐ THE EXCHANGES

Trader

Traders are skillful, aggressive negotiators who can handle millions of dollars in securities annually. There are two basic kinds of traders—those who work over a bank of phones at a trading desk in an office and those who work on the floor of an exchange.

Many bond and OTC traders work by phone with traders at other broker-dealers.

Transaction prices are negotiated by the traders. Their goal is to negotiate the most advantageous price possible in each transaction. In most firms, traders trade for the firm's account as well as for customers. A successful trader must have a good sense of where the market is and where it is headed.

Floor traders are the people you see whenever television shows the floor of the stock exchange. They are stationed on the floor of the exchange and trade securities through an open outcry auction. After arriving at a price, they swap small pieces of paper (tickets) that confirm the trade. Runners then carry the tickets to the broker-dealer's desk on the floor. The information is relayed from the floor desk back to the firm and eventually to the customer.

Many firms derive substantial revenues from their trading activities. Both floor traders and desk ("upstairs") traders have the ability to generate significant profits (or losses!) for their firms. They can seek out creative ways to maximize returns in the short-term market. They take risks in the hope of making profits.

Specialist

A specialist is a special kind of trader. The specialist trades in specific stocks assigned by the exchange. The specialist's chief function is to maintain an orderly market in the stocks assigned to him by buying or selling shares as a principal to fill gaps in the market. The securities handled by the specialist are allocated by the exchanges based on each firm's trading ability.

Specialists' earnings are based on the commissions and trading profits they generate.

Messenger and Runner

The term "runner" is a generic term describing a person in the securities industry who transports documents from place to place. The securities industry creates massive amounts of paper, which often needs to get from place to place quickly. Each firm employs its own runners (or couriers) to transport the documents. Some runners work on the floor of the exchange or between the floor and the member firm's offices. Others work internally in the member firm's offices. Outside messenger services are used to shuttle between member firms, picking up and delivering checks and securities.

Floor Clerk

The floor clerical staff work at the member firm's trading desk on the floor. They receive incoming orders and get them to the runners for the floor traders. When an order is filled, the clerical staff ensure that the firm and the NYSE are notified of the trade. At the end of the trading day, the floor clerical staff must ensure that all orders entered are accounted for, and that those left unfilled are filed according to the instructions on the order.

Many people, particularly college students interested in summer jobs, begin their careers in the securities industry as clerks and runners on the floor of an exchange. Some eventually move to trading and market making, others into sales or other work off the floor. No matter which course they take, time spent on the floor of an exchange is an invaluable learning experience.

☐ SALES MANAGEMENT

Branch Manager

Many broker-dealers have branch offices in addition to their main office. This network allows brokers to live and work near their customers, and gives firms the ability to reach a wider market. Modern communications means that a broker in a distant branch has the same access to the floor of the exchange as one right on Wall Street. To ensure smooth operation of their branches and compliance with SEC and exchange rules, broker-dealers employ branch managers.

The branch manager's role is four-fold. A manager must:

- **Function as a leader to the salespeople in the branch.** This entails assisting them in setting objectives, providing them with sales ideas, helping them to solve problems and providing appropriate training.
- **Recruit, select and train new brokers.** Broker-dealers are always looking for the right people. The branch manager is the point-person in this search. The manager must seek out potential candidates, either from other firms or from people outside the industry. After finding them, the manager must ensure that they meet the firm's employment requirements and then provide a basic level of training.
- **Manage the staff and the office.** Branch offices are a microcosm of the head office. The branch offices carry on many of the functions of the head office of the broker-dealer, only at a smaller level. The branch manager must maintain the office, ensure that there are adequate and properly trained staff, and ensure that costs are properly contained.
- **Monitor and ensure compliance with regulations.** Branch managers are responsible for compliance in the branch. Failure to discharge this responsibility properly could result in their removal from branch management and possibly in disciplinary action or even censure. This is the most important supervision responsibility in their job.

The branch manager's role is a varied one, with many different things going on in an average day. They are usually paid through a combination of commission on trades made by their own customers (if they are permitted to maintain their own book of business), a salary from the firm, and a percentage of the profits at their branch. Even though the compensation may be less than that of a very successful broker, many salespeople look to branch management as a career opportunity—a step towards upper level management.

Securities Principals

If anyone associated with a member will be managing or supervising the member's investment banking or securities business, that person must be registered as a *principal* with the NASD. This includes those people involved in training associated persons and in soliciting business. Unless the member firm is a sole proprietorship, there must be at least two *registered principals* per firm, one of whom must be registered as a General Securities Principal (Series 24).

Following are descriptions of some of the principals licenses you may encounter in a securities firm.

Registered Options Principal (Series 4). The Series 4 is the Registered Options Principal (ROP) qualification examination. This license entitles the principal to supervise a broker-dealer's options business and the registered representatives who sell options. If the member firm does options business with the public, there must be at least one ROP in that firm.

Each broker-dealer that does public business in options must also designate a Senior Registered Options Principal (SROP) and a Compliance Registered Options Principal (CROP) to supervise and review options accounts.

General Securities Sales Supervisor (Series 8). The Series 8 is the General Securities Sales Supervisor license. This license entitles the principal to supervise the sales of all types of securities products. The NYSE requires a Series 8-qualified principal to be in charge of a member's branch offices and sales activities. Most branch managers of NYSE firms have a Series 8 license. This is the most comprehensive of the sales supervision principal licenses available and requires the Series 7 as a prerequisite.

General Securities Principal (Series 24). A Series 24 General Securities Principal license allows a principal to supervise a member firm's investment banking, trading and market-making, brokerage office operations and compliance with applicable financial responsibility rules. This is the most comprehensive of the NASD principal licenses available and requires the Series 7 as a prerequisite.

Investment Company/Variable Contract Products Limited Principal (Series 26). The Series 26 registration allows a principal to supervise a broker-dealer's mutual fund and variable annuity business and sales. Many firms specializing in mutual funds and insurance license a number of Series 26 principals. Both the Series 6 and the Series 7 can serve as prerequisites for the Series 26.

Financial and Operations Principal (Series 27). In addition to having at least one General Securities Principal, each member must have at least one Financial and Operations Principal (FinOp). The FinOp oversees the keeping and preservation of records, net capital, uniform practice rules, financial reporting and Federal Reserve Board requirements of a member. There are no prerequisite licenses a candidate must acquire before sitting for the Series 27.

Introducing Broker-Dealer Financial and Operations Principal (Series 28). Each introducing broker-dealer must have at least one Introducing Broker-Dealer Financial and Operations Principal. The Series 28 principal oversees the same parts of a member's business as the Series 27 principal but, because the member firm introduces its accounts to a clearing member, the Series 28 principal does not have as many record-keeping requirements. There are no prerequisites a candidate has to meet before sitting for the Series 28.

Direct Participation Programs Limited Principal (Series 39). The Series 39 Direct Participation Programs Limited Principal license entitles the principal to supervise a member's oil and gas, real estate, motion picture and other types of limited partnership business and is used by many firms selling direct investment limited partnership products. The Series 7 or the Series 22 can serve as a prerequisite for the Series 39.

Municipal Securities Principal (Series 53). The Series 53 Municipal Securities Principal license entitles the principal to supervise the MSRB member's municipal and government securities business and is used by many firms selling municipal debt products. The Series 7 or the Series 52 can serve as a prerequisite for the Series 53.

□ SALES

Wholesaler

There are many different financial products with a wide range of features and benefits, and more are being created each year. The task of keeping up with new products and new developments of existing products would take up all of the hours in the day for the average registered representative, leaving no time to develop business. Fortunately, the securities industry employs a specialized type of salesperson known as a *wholesaler* to make the flow of new product information to the sales force more effective.

Wholesalers are employed by brokerage firms, investment bankers, mutual funds, limited partnerships, insurance companies and others that package or offer investment products. The wholesaler's job is to market the company's products to the firms and registered representatives who will sell them to the public.

A wholesaler's job involves extensive travel. A typical wholesaler travels from branch to branch or firm to firm for three or more weeks out of every month in the course of promoting a particular investment or idea. In an average day, a wholesaler may visit several different offices, often at different firms, making presentations to brokers, both individually and as a group. A wholesaler will schedule a meeting with registered representatives to discuss the features and benefits of the product and to answer any questions they might have. He must be an expert not only in the technical aspects of the product he represents, but also in how to sell it. Wholesalers frequently work with representatives to put on seminars for customers featuring the products they represent.

Companies that offer a specific packaged product (such as a mutual fund company) usually employ wholesalers in every region in which they sell. Broker-dealers also employ in-house wholesalers to train the firms' representatives on the various proprietary products created and handled by the firms.

Institutional Registered Representative

The job of the institutional registered representative is similar to that of a retail registered representative, but on a larger scale. These brokers deal with large institutions, corporations, pension plans and portfolios. As with retail registered representatives, they suggest investments, place orders, provide quotes and offer services to customers. The primary difference is one of scale—institutional brokers deal in larger accounts than do retail brokers.

Most retail registered representatives talk to their customers on an irregular basis, occasionally as often as once or twice a day, but sometimes only once or twice a month. Institutional brokers must be in contact with their customers more frequently, even to the point of making hourly telephone calls to the account.

Because institutional registered representatives work with larger accounts and trades, they often negotiate pricing of securities and commissions. Negotiating skills take time to develop and can mean the difference between large profits and losses. Because their customers are usually investment professionals with research staffs of their own, institutional brokers often tend to focus more on trading tactics and less on selling ideas to customers.

Institutional registered representatives usually have extensive staff support. They are expected to have a high level of knowledge of markets and the economy in general.

Retail Registered Representative

The registered representative (also known as a *financial consultant, account executive* and *customer representative*) is an important part of the brokerage business. The basic role of the registered representative is to assist customers by placing their buy and sell orders, handling inquiries, giving them price quotes, providing them with investment advice, monitoring their accounts and performing numerous other services for them.

Much of the registered representative's work is done over the phone. Different firms require different types of registered representatives. The NASD, NYSE, MSRB and NFA each offers qualifications examinations for various representative specializations. Among these are the following.

National Commodities Futures Representative (Series 3). The Series 3 is the National Commodity Futures Exam. This license entitles the representative to sell commodities futures and is used by many firms selling primarily commodities-related products, including managed commodities accounts and commodities mutual funds.

Investment Company/Variable Contract Products Limited Representative (Series 6). The Series 6 is the Investment Company/Variable Contract Products Limited Representative license. This license entitles the representative to sell mutual funds and variable annuities and is used by many firms selling primarily insurance-related products. It can serve as the prerequisite for the Series 26.

General Securities Representative (Series 7). A Series 7 General Securities Registered Representative license allows a registered representative to sell all types of securities products, though not commodities futures (which requires a Series 3). This is the most comprehensive of the NASD/NYSE representative licenses available and serves as a prerequisite for most of the NASD's principals examinations.

Direct Participation Programs Limited Representative (Series 22). The Series 22 Direct Participation Programs Limited Representative license entitles the representative to sell oil and gas, real estate, motion picture and other types of limited partnerships. It can serve as a prerequisite for the Series 39.

Municipal Securities Representative (Series 52). The Series 52 Municipal Securities Representative license entitles the representative to sell municipal and government securities. It can serve as a prerequisite for the Series 53.

Corporate Securities Limited Representative (Series 62). The Series 62 Corporate Securities Limited Representative license entitles the representative to sell all types of corporate securities, but not municipal securities, options, direct participation programs or a limited number of other products. It is used by many firms selling general securities products that want to limit their representatives to corporate securities. The Series 62 can serve as a prerequisite for the Series 24.

Uniform Securities Agent State Law Exam (Series 63). The Series 63 Uniform Securities Agent State Law Exam (USASLE) license is required by many states in addition to a registered representative's primary license. The exam, promulgated by the North American Securities Administrators Association (NASAA), is intended to educate registered representatives about state laws, help state administrators gauge the knowledge of new agents and serve in place of multiple state-level exams. There are no prerequisites for the Series 63.

Uniform Investment Adviser (Series 65). The Series 65 Uniform Investment Adviser license is required by many states for anyone who wishes to register as an investment adviser or who offers investment advice as a regular part of his normal business and is typically required in addition to a registered representative's primary license. Requirements for licensing differ from state to state, but there are no prerequisites for the Series 65.

Sales Assistant

The sales assistant acts as an extension of a registered representative. It is the job of the sales assistant to handle certain aspects of the registered representative's work so that the representative can function more effectively. This typically involves matching orders with execution reports, confirming filled orders back to customers, providing quotes over the phone, arranging appointments, updating customer records and handling all manner of customer requests.

If properly licensed, the sales assistant may even be involved in entering orders from customers. Some firms require sales assistants to take the licensing exams even before starting the job just to meet this need. A properly registered sales assistant can even convey investment advice from the registered representative to customers.

Most sales assistants are paid a basic salary, and some get a portion of their registered representatives' earnings by way of a bonus. Many times the representative will pay all or a part of the assistant's salary. As a way of reducing costs, some representatives will share an assistant; the assistant will work with two, three, four representatives or more. Sharing is most common where the firm hires and pays for the assistant.

☐ ETHICS IN THE SECURITIES INDUSTRY

"Ethics is for keeps."
Richard C. Breeden, SEC Chairman

The securities industry is a highly competitive business. It is a business where, at times, the participants' desire to succeed may seem to outweigh all other considerations. Despite the enormous personal pressure to succeed, the securities industry is governed by a very strong code of ethics. There is agreement on what constitutes acceptable behavior, and those who engage in unacceptable behavior risk sanctions ranging from fines and reprimands all the way up to expulsion from the industry. There are clear standards against which business behavior and practices are measured for fairness and equity.

A problem in evaluating ethical behavior in securities transactions is the speed at which the industry operates. Decisions are made in split seconds, transactions occur almost instantaneously and millions of pieces of paper are generated and handled daily. If there are questions about the propriety of a transaction or an agreement, it is nearly impossible to address them before the fact. But, addressed they will be!

Securities industry regulators are very active in detecting and preventing unethical behavior. Investigators regularly examine activity at all levels—from large firms to individual investors. Even the most junior of employees is expected to employ high standards of business ethics and commercial honor in dealing with the public, customers, the firm and the industry.

Corporate Ethics and Responsibility

The rules that guide the relationships between members of the securities industry and all of the other participants are set by the SEC, NASD, NYSE, MSRB and other regulatory bodies and exchanges throughout the country. The federal securities acts, such as the Securities Act of 1933 and the Securities Exchange Act of 1934, the *NASD Manual*, the NYSE Constitution and Rules, and the various legislative acts governing securities all contain guidelines for what is and what is not acceptable behavior. It is the responsibility of securities firms to be familiar with and follow these guidelines.

Advertising and marketing by securities industry members must comply with industry guidelines. Important among these guidelines is the rule that representations to the public must not understate the risks or overstate the profit potential of an investment.

There is more to corporate responsibility than complying with rules, however. An important responsibility of any corporation, including a broker-dealer, is to its stockholders. Broker-dealers must be profitable if they are to provide the long-term stability and security needed for a strong, viable securities market.

Members of the industry must also treat their employees with honesty and fairness. Firms are responsible for rewarding those who contribute to the success. The rules of employment must be clear, and the need for ethical behavior must be emphasized.

One part of corporate responsibility for ethical behavior involves a commitment to self-regulation. Individuals within the firm who engage in unethical behavior must be detected and their behavior corrected or risk being removed from their jobs. Compliance departments are generally the center of member firms' continuing effort to self-police. Employees need to know that compliance with regulations is important to the firm, and that noncompliance is dealt with swiftly.

Through self-regulation, broker-dealers protect customers. Protecting customers includes ensuring that they are fully informed about their investments, have access to the information they need to make good investment decisions, and receive value for the commissions and markup paid to brokers and dealers. Customers deserve fair and equitable treatment. Without this, the industry would lose credibility, the trust of the public and, ultimately, its existence.

Employee Ethics and Responsibility

The NASD Rules of Fair Practice and other regulations cover employees as well. All those who work for a broker-dealer represent the firm in all that they do. Employees, both producers and nonproducers, are responsible for ensuring that their activities fall within the guidelines set by regulators and by their firms.

Many firms view the regulations as minimum standards and set stricter policies for internal behavior. Employees are responsible for knowing their firms' policies as they relate to the jobs they do.

Even a well-intentioned employee of a broker-dealer can sometimes run afoul of the regulations. As an example, a customer might suggest that an employee deliver a security in person, saving the firm the time and expense of registered mail delivery. Doing this might seem like a good idea; but in most firms, delivering securities in this fashion is strictly against policy, and any person doing so could be subject to dismissal. Shortcuts are rarely a good idea—policies and regulations protect the employee, firm and customer.

Investment recommendations must be in keeping with customer needs and objectives. Customers should be guided to investments that make sense for them, not just for the broker. Every investment should be fully explained, and the explanation should include a discussion of the investment's risks. At no time should a customer knowingly be encouraged to own an investment that could put him at risk beyond his financial capacity.

Customers also expect and deserve a high level of confidentiality. Employees of broker-dealers may never divulge personal information about customers without the express permission of the customers. This includes such information as security positions, personal and financial details and trading intentions. The securities industry depends on the trust of its customers. The employee is responsible for meeting and keeping that trust.

Employees have a responsibility to the industry as well. Serving on industry committees, public education, and self-education are all part of service to the industry, as is representing one's firm and the industry in community activities.

Customer Ethics and Responsibility

Insider trading is a basic violation of industry regulations. This and other practices that would tend to give select investors an unfair advantage over the general public are prohibited by regulation. It is the responsibility of the individual investor to abide by those regulations.

It is up to the customer to make a full and honest disclosure of her investment wishes and requirements to the registered representative. This information is all the registered representative has on which to base recommendations. Such information may also be important in gaining permission to engage in specific kinds or sizes of trades. A customer who hides key facts or fails to disclose relevant information could jeopardize the registered representative's career. Failure to provide information is often the first signal to compliance departments of potential trouble.

□ REVIEW

Check how well you have learned the information contained in this chapter by completing the following sentences.

Human resources, payroll, marketing, compliance, legal and other nonsales departments are collectively known as a brokerage firm's

_____

(See page 172)

The regulatory department within each brokerage firm is known as the

_____

(See page 175)

Advertising and sales literature is designed, created, filed with the appropriate SRO and issued by the

_____

(See page 176)

Hiring, training, insurance, employee records and other functions are handled by the

_____

(See page 177)

The traders employed by member firms to make a market in stocks assigned to them by an exchange are known as

_____

(See page 178)

The person who works as a courier for a brokerage firm or an exchange, moving important orders and documents within and between companies, is also known as

_____

(See page 179)

The branch manager's four main functions are

_____

(See page 180)

A person who will be involved in managing and supervising a member firm's investment banking or securities business must be registered as

_____

(See page 181)

The person who markets a firm's products to registered reps, answers their questions and helps them sell those products to the public is the

_____

(See page 183)

The person responsible for assisting individual customers with investment decisions, placing orders, providing them with advice and giving them quotes is the

_____

(See page 185)

The person who works directly with one or more registered reps, arranging appointments, handling customer inquiries and updating customer records, is the rep's

_____

(See page 186)

Glossary

abandon The act of not exercising or selling an option before its expiration.

accredited investor Generally accepted to be an investor who:
- has a net worth of $1 million or more; or
- has had an annual income of $200,000 or more in each of the two most recent years (or $300,000 jointly with a spouse) and who has a reasonable expectation of reaching the same income level in the current year.

actual The physical commodity being traded, as opposed to the futures contracts on that commodity.

advertisement Any material designed for use by newspapers, magazines, radio, television, telephone recording or any other public medium to solicit business.

agency issue A debt security issued by an authorized agency of the federal government. Such issues are backed by the issuing agencies themselves, not by the full faith and credit of the U.S. government (except GNMA and Export-Import Bank).

agency transaction A transaction in which the broker-dealer is acting for the accounts of others by buying or selling securities on behalf of customers; also, securities sold through normal broker transactions, executed through a national dealer market.

agent (1) An individual acting for the accounts of others; any person licensed by a state as a life insurance agent. (*Syn.* broker) (2) A securities salesperson who represents a broker-dealer or an issuer when selling or trying to sell securities to the investing public. This individual is considered an agent whether he actually receives or simply solicits orders. In other words, an agent is a registered representative or anyone who receives an order while representing a broker-dealer.

aggressive Investment strategy A method of investing a person uses when trying to get the maximum return on a portfolio by timing purchases and sales to coincide with expected market movements and by varying the structure of the portfolio in line with these expected market moves.

AMBAC The AMBAC Indemnity Corporation offers insurance on the timely payment of interest and principal obligations of municipal securities. Bonds insured by AMBAC usually receive an AAA rating from the rating services.

American depositary receipt (ADR) A negotiable receipt for a given number of shares of stock in a foreign corporation. An ADR is bought and sold in the U.S. securities markets just as stock is traded.

American Stock Exchange AUTOAMOS The American Stock Exchange uses the Automatic AMEX Options Switch (AUTOAMOS) system for op-

tions orders. AUTOAMOS can be used to electronically route day, GTC and marketable limit orders from brokers to AMEX specialists and execution reports from the specialists back to the brokers.

American Stock Exchange AUTOPER The American Stock Exchange uses the Automatic Post Execution & Reporting (AUTOPER) system for equity orders. AUTOPER can be used to electronically route day, GTC and marketable limit orders from brokers to AMEX specialists and execution reports from the specialists back to the brokers.

amortization Paying off debt (principal) over a period of time in periodic installments. Amortization is also defined as the ratable deduction of certain capitalized expenditures over a specified period of time.

annultant A person who receives the distribution of an annuity contract.

annuity A contract between an insurance company and an individual, which generally guarantees lifetime income to the person on whose life the contract is based in return for either a lump sum or a periodic payment to the insurance company.

appreciation The increase in value of an asset.

ask The current price for which a security may be bought, as in the OTC market. For mutual funds, the asked price includes any sales charge that is added to the net asset value. (*Syn.* bid, offer)

asset Anything that an individual or a corporation owns.

assignment (1) A document accompanying or part of a stock certificate that is signed by the person named on the certificate for the purpose of transferring the certificate's title to another person's name. (2) The act of identifying and notifying an account holder that an option held short in that account has been exercised by the option owner.

associated person of a member (AP) Any employee, manager, director, officer or partner of a member broker-dealer or another entity (issuer, bank, etc.) or any person controlling, controlled by or in common control with that member.

at-the-money An option in which the underlying stock is trading precisely at the exercise price of that option.

auction market A market in which buyers enter competitive bids and sellers enter competitive offers simultaneously. The NYSE is an auction market. (*Syn.* double-auction market)

authorized stock The number of shares of stock that a corporation is permitted to issue. This number is stipulated in the corporation's state-approved charter and may be changed by a vote of the corporation's stockholders.

balanced fund A type of mutual fund whose stated investment policy is to have at all times some portion of its investment assets in bonds as well as in common stock. Therefore, there is a balance between the two classes, equity and debt.

balance of payments An international accounting record of all payments made from one nation to another.

balance sheet A report of a company's financial condition at a specific time.

banker's acceptance A money-market instrument used to finance international and domestic trade. A banker's acceptance is a check drawn on a bank by an importer or exporter of goods and represents the bank's conditional promise to pay the face amount of the note at maturity (normally less than three months).

bear market A market in which prices of securities are falling or are expected to fall.

bid An indication by an investor, a trader or a dealer of a willingness to buy a security or commodity at a particular price.

block trade A trade of 10,000 or more shares.

blue chip stock The issues of normally strong, well-established companies that have demonstrated their ability to pay dividends in good and bad times.

Blue List, The A daily trade publication for the secondary market that lists the current municipal bond offerings of banks and brokers nationwide.

blue-sky laws The nickname for state regulations governing the securities industry.

bond An evidence of debt issued by corporations, municipalities and the federal government. Bonds represent the borrowing of money by a corporation or government. A bond is a legal obligation of the issuing company or government to repay principal at the maturity of the bond. Terms of the repayment and any interest to be paid are stated in the bond indenture. Bonds are issued with a par value ($1,000) representing the amount of money borrowed. The issuer promises to pay a percentage of the par value as interest on the borrowed funds. The interest payment is stated on the face of the bond at issue.

bond fund A type of mutual fund whose investment policy is to provide stable income with modest capital risks. It invests in corporate, government or municipal bonds. Some corporate bond funds include preferred stock.

bond quote A corporate bond that is quoted on a percentage of par with increments of 1/8, where a quote of 99 1/8 represents 99.125% of par ($1,000), or $991.25. Bonds may also be quoted on a yield to maturity basis.

bond ratio The percentage of a company's invested capital that is provided by long-term debt financing. It is found by dividing the face value of the outstanding bonds by the invested capital. (*Syn.* debt ratio)

book-entry security A security sold without delivery of a certificate. Evidence of ownership is maintained on records kept by a central agency, such as the Treasury on the sale of Treasury bills. Transfer of ownership is recorded by entering the change on the books.

book value per share A measure of the net worth of each share of common stock that is calculated by subtracting intangible assets and preferred stock from total net worth and then dividing by the number of shares of common out-

standing. (*Syn.* net tangible assets per common share)

branch office Any location identified by any means to the public as a location in which the member conducts securities business.

broker (1) An individual or a firm that charges a fee or commission for executing buy and sell orders submitted by another individual or firm. (2) The role of a brokerage firm when it acts as an agent for a customer and charges the customer for its services.

bull market A market in which prices of securities are moving or are expected to move higher.

business day A day on which the markets are open for business (trading).

buying power The dollar amount of securities that a client can purchase without depositing additional cash or securities.

call An option contract giving the owner the right to buy stock at a stated price within a specified period of time.

callable bond A type of bond issued with a provision allowing the issuer to redeem the bond prior to maturity at a predetermined price.

callable preferred stock A type of preferred stock carrying the provision that the corporation retains the right to call in the stock at a certain price and retire it.

call provision The written agreement between an issuing corporation and its bondholders or preferred stockholders, giving the corporation the option to redeem its senior securities at a specified price before maturity and under specified conditions.

capital Accumulated money or goods used to produce income.

capital appreciation A rise in the market prices of assets owned.

capital gain The gain (selling price minus cost basis) on an asset.

capitalization The sum of a company's long-term debt, capital stock and surpluses. (*Syn.* invested capital)

capital loss The loss (cost basis minus selling price) on an asset.

capital market That segment of the securities market that deals in instruments with more than one year to maturity—that is, long-term debt and equity securities.

capital stock The total stated value or par value of all outstanding preferred stock and common stock of a corporation.

capital structure The composition of long-term funds (equity and debt) a company has as a source for financing.

cash account An account in which a client pays in full for securities purchased.

cash commodity The actual, physical good being traded, rather than a futures contract on that good.

cash dividend A cash payment to a company's stockholders out of the company's current earnings or accumulated profits. The dividend must be declared by the board of directors.

cashiering department The department within a brokerage firm that delivers and receives securities and money to and from other firms and clients of the firm. (*Syn.* security cage)

cash market Transactions between buyers and sellers of commodi-ties that entail immediate delivery of and payment for a physical commodity. (*Syn.* cash-and-carry market)

chartist A securities analyst who uses charts and graphs of the past price movements of a security to predict its future movements.

Chicago Board Options Exchange (CBOE) The first national securities exchange for the trading of listed options.

churning Excessive trading in a customer's account. The term suggests that the registered representative ignores the objectives and interests of clients and stimulates trading to increase commissions. (*Syn.* overtrading)

clearing agency An agency that acts as an intermediary between the sides in a securities transaction, receiving and delivering payments and securities. Any organization that fills this function, including a securities depository but not including a Federal Reserve Bank, is considered a clearing agency.

clearing broker A broker-dealer that clears its own trades, as well as trades of introducing brokers. A clearing broker-dealer can hold customers' securities and cash. (*Syn.* carrying broker)

close The price of the last transaction for a particular security on a particular day; the midprice of a closing trading range.

closed-end management company A management investment company operated in much the same manner as a conventional corporation. The closed-end fund will issue a fixed number of shares for sale (fixed capitalization). The shares may be of several classes. Shares are bought and sold in the secondary market; the fund does not offer to redeem shares. The market price of the shares is determined by supply and demand and not by their net asset value. The shares may be traded on an exchange or in the over-the-counter market.

Code of Arbitration Provides a method of handling securities-related disputes or clearing controversies between members, public customers, clearing corporations or clearing banks. Any claim, dispute or controversy subject to arbitration is required to be submitted to arbitration.

Code of Procedure The NASD's procedure for handling trade practice complaints. The NASD District Business Conduct Committee (DBCC) is the first body to hear and judge complaints. Appeals and review of DBCC decisions are handled by the NASD Board of Governors.

combined account A customer account that has cash and long and short margin positions in different securities.

commercial paper An unsecured, short-term promissory note issued by well-known businesses chiefly for financing accounts receivable. It is usually issued at a discount reflecting prevailing market interest rates. Maturities range up to 270 days.

commission broker A member eligible to execute orders for customers of a member firm on the floor of the Exchange. (*Syn.* floor broker)

Committee on Uniform Securities Identification Procedures (CUSIP) A committee that assigns identification numbers and codes to all securities, to be used when recording buy and sell orders.

Commodities Futures Trading Commission (CFTC) The federal regulatory agency established by the Commodities Futures Trading Commission Act of 1974 to administer the Commodities Exchange Act. The five CFTC commissioners are appointed by the President (subject to Senate approval).

commodity Any bulk good traded on an exchange or in the cash (spot) market, such as metals, grains, meats and so on.

Commodity Exchange Authority (CEA) The predecessor of the Commodities Futures Trading Commission established by the U.S. Department of Agriculture to administer the Commodities Exchange Act of 1936.

common stock An equity security that represents ownership in a corporation. This is the first security a corporation issues to raise capital.

competitive bidding The submission of sealed bids by rival underwriting syndicates that want the privilege of underwriting the issue of securities. Competitive bidding normally is used to determine the underwriters for issues of general obligation municipal bonds and is required by law in most states for general obligation bonds of more than $100,000.

confirmation A bill or comparison of trade that is sent or given to a customer on or before the settlement date.

Consolidated Quotation System (CQS) The NASD's quotation and last-sale reporting service for NASD members that are active market makers of listed securities in the third market. As a quotations collection system, CQS is used by market makers that are willing to stand ready to buy and sell the securities for their own accounts on a continuous basis, but that do not wish to do so through an exchange.

CQS is part of the NASDAQ market-making system. Quotation display service is available to all NASDAQ subscribers (at a fee), while quotation input service is available only to those members that are registered to do business in third-market stocks. NASD members that are registered market makers may enter quotes into CQS through the NASDAQ system.

Consolidated Tape Also known as the *Consolidated Ticker Tape*, a service of the NYSE designed to deliver real-time reports of securities transactions to subscribers as they occur on the various exchanges. Subscribers to the Tape can choose to receive transaction reports in either of two ways: over the high-speed electronic line (directly linked to their Quotrons® or other types of terminals); or through the low-speed ticker (visible report) line—the type of report commonly seen as quotes racing across a sign at a brokerage counter.

Consumer Price Index (CPI) A measure of inflation or deflation based on price changes in consumer goods and services.

contingent-deferred sales load A sales load that is charged upon redemption of mutual fund shares or variable contracts; also called a *back-end load*. The load is charged on a declining basis annually, usually reduced to zero after an extended holding period (up to eight years).

contract One unit of trading in options or futures.

convertible bond A type of debt security (usually in the form of a debenture) that can be converted into (exchanged for) equity securities of the issuing corporation—that is, common or preferred stock.

convertible preferred stock A type of preferred stock that offers the holder the privilege of exchanging (converting) the preferred stock for (into) common stock at specified prices or rates. Dividends may be cumulative or noncumulative.

cooling-off period The period (a minimum of 20 days) between the filing date of a registration statement and the effective date of the registration. In practice, this period varies in length.

corporation A form of business organization in which the total worth of the organization is divided into shares of stock, each share representing a unit of ownership. By law, the corporation has certain rights and responsibilities. It is characterized by a continuous life span and the limited liability of the owners.

coupon bond A bond without the name of the owner printed on its face and with coupons representing semiannual interest payments attached. Coupons are submitted to the trustee by the holder to receive the interest payments. (*Syn.* bearer bond)

covenant A promise or restriction of an issuer made part of a trust indenture (bond contract). Examples include rate covenants that establish a minimum revenue coverage for a bond; insurance covenants that require insurance on a project; and maintenance covenants that require maintenance on a facility constructed with the proceeds of a bond issue.

credit agreement An agreement signed in conjunction with a margin agreement, outlining the conditions of the credit arrangement between broker and client.

credit balance (CR) The amount of money remaining in a client's account after all commitments have been paid in full. (*Syn.* credit record, credit register)

cumulative preferred stock A type of preferred stock that offers the holder any unpaid dividends in arrears. These dividends accumulate and must be paid to the holder of cumulative preferred stock before any dividends can be paid to the common stockholders.

cumulative voting rights A voting procedure that permits stockholders to cast all of their votes for any one director or to cast their total number of votes in any proportion they choose.

current market value (CMV) The current market price of the securities in an account, based on the closing prices on the previous

business day. (*Syn.* long market value)

current yield The annual dollar return on a security (interest or dividends) divided by the current market price of the security (bonds or stock).

custodian The institution or person responsible for protecting the property of another. Mutual funds have custodians responsible for safeguarding certificates and performing clerical duties.

custodian of a minor One who manages a gift of securities to a minor under the Uniform Gifts to Minors Act; also, someone who takes charge of an incompetent's affairs.

customer Any person or other entity that transacts business with a firm.

customer statement A statement of a customer's account showing positions and entries. The SEC requires that a customer statement be sent quarterly, but customers generally receive them monthly.

dated date The date on which interest on a bond issue begins to accrue.

day order An order that is canceled if it is not executed on the day it is entered.

day trader A trader in securities or commodities who opens all positions after the opening of the market and offsets or closes out all positions before the close of the market on the same day.

dealer The role of a brokerage firm when it acts as a principal in a particular trade. A firm is acting as a dealer when it buys or sells a security for its own account and at its own risk and then charges the customer a markup or markdown. Any person who is engaged in the business of buying and selling securities for her own account either directly or through a broker is considered a dealer. (*Syn.* principal)

debenture A debt obligation backed by the general credit of the issuing corporation.

debit balance (DR) The amount of money a client owes a brokerage firm.

debt security An evidence of debt issued by corporations, municipalities or the federal government.

declaration date The date on which a company declares an upcoming dividend.

defensive industry An industry that is relatively unaffected by business cycles, such as the food industry or the utilities industry.

deferred annuity An annuity contract that guarantees that payment of income, installment payments or a lump-sum payment will be made at an agreed upon future time.

deficiency letter A list of additions or corrections that must be made to a registration statement before the SEC will release an offering to the public. The SEC sends a deficiency letter to the issuing corporation. (*Syn.* bedbug letter)

deflation A persistent fall in the general level of prices.

demand Consumers' desire and willingness to pay for a particular good or service.

dilution A reduction in earnings per share of common stock. Dilution occurs through the issuance of additional shares of common stock and the conversion of convertible securities.

direct participation program (DPP) A program that provides for flow-through tax consequences, regardless of the structure of the legal entity or the vehicle for distribution. These programs include but are not limited to oil and gas programs, real estate programs, agricultural programs, cattle programs, condominium securities, Subchapter S corporate offerings and all other programs of a similar nature, regardless of the industry represented by the program.

discount The difference between the price paid for a security and the security's face amount at issue.

discount bond A bond selling below par.

discretionary account An account in which the principal (beneficial owner) has given a registered representative authority to make transactions in the account at the registered representative's discretion.

disposable income (DI) The sum that people divide between spending and personal savings.

diversified management company A management company that has at least 75% of its total assets in cash, receivables or securities invested, no more than 5% of its total assets invested in the voting securities of any company, and no single investment representing ownership of more than 10% of the outstanding voting securities of any one company.

dividend A distribution of the earnings of a corporation. Dividends may be in the form of cash, stock or property (securities owned by a corporation). The board of directors must declare a dividend before it can be paid.

dividend yield The annual percentage of return that an investor receives on either common or preferred stock. The yield is based on the amount of the annual dividend divided by the market price of the stock.

Dow Jones Industrial Average (DJIA) The most widely used market indicator, composed of 30 large, actively traded and well-known issues.

due diligence The careful investigation by the underwriters that is necessary to ensure that all material information pertinent to an issue has been disclosed to the public.

due diligence meeting A meeting between an issuing corporation's officials and representatives of the underwriting group held to discuss details of the pending issue of securities. These details include the registration statement and the preparation of prospectuses.

earnings per share (EPS) The net income of a corporation divided by the number of shares of common stock outstanding.

economic risk The risk related to international developments and domestic events.

EE savings bond A nonnegotiable government debt issued at a discount from face value. The difference between the purchase price and the value of the bond upon re-

demption represents the interest earned.

effective date The date the registration of an issue of securities becomes effective. The underwriter confirms sales of the newly issued securities after this date.

efficient market theory A theory based on the assumption that the stock market processes information efficiently. This theory postulates that new information, as it becomes known, is reflected immediately in the price of stock and, therefore, stock prices represent fair prices.

elasticity The responsiveness of consumers and producers to a change in prices. A large change in demand or production resulting from a small change in price for a good would be considered an indication of elasticity. A small or no change in production or demand following a change in price would be considered an indication of inelasticity.

Employee Retirement Income Security Act (ERISA) A 1974 law governing the operation of most private pension and benefit plans. The law eased pension eligibility rules, set up the Pension Benefit Guaranty Corporation and established guidelines for the management of pension funds.

equity The ownership interest of common and preferred stockholders in a corporation; also, the client's net worth in a margin account; also, what is owned less what is owed.

equity financing When stock (common or preferred) is sold to individuals or institutions and, in return for the money paid, the individuals or institutions receive ownership interest in the corporation.

equity interest (1) When used with respect to a corporation: common stock and any security convertible into, exchangeable for or exercisable for common stock. (2) When used with respect to a partnership: an interest in the capital or profits or losses of the partnership.

equity security According to SEC definition, any:

- stock or similar security;
- certificate of participation in any profit-sharing agreement;
- preorganization certificate, subscription, transferable share, voting trust certificate or certificate of deposit for an equity security;
- limited partnership interest, interest in a joint venture or certificate of interest in a business trust;
- convertible security, warrant or rights certificate that carries the right to subscribe to an equity security; or
- put, call or other option that offers the privilege of buying or selling an equity security.

If the market price of a security trends or tracks with the price of the common stock, it is an equity security.

Eurobond A bond issued by a government or corporation in a particular European country and denominated in that country's currency but sold outside that country.

Eurodollar U.S. currency held in European banks outside the United States.

exchange Any organization, association or group of persons that maintains or provides a marketplace in which securities can be bought and sold. An exchange does not have to be a physical place, and several strictly electronic exchanges do business in this country.

exchange-listed security In order for a security to be traded by exchange members on an exchange, it has to be listed on an exchange. Once it is accepted for listing, it is admitted to full trading privileges on that exchange.

exchange rate The price at which one country's currency can be converted into that of another.

exempt security A security exempt from the registration requirements (although not from the antifraud requirements) of the Securities Act of 1933 (e.g., U.S. government and municipal securities).

exercise To implement the rights of an option or a warrant (e.g., a call holder exercises a call by implementing the right to buy at least 100 shares of the underlying stock at the agreed upon price).

exercise price The price per share at which the holder of a call, an option or a warrant may buy (or the holder of a put may sell) the underlying security. (*Syn.* strike price, striking price)

expiration date The specified date on which an option becomes worthless and the buyer no longer has the rights specified in the contract.

ex-rights Stock purchased without rights.

ex-rights date The date on or after which stocks will be traded without subscription rights.

ex-warrants date The date on or after which the buyer of a security is no longer entitled to warrants that will be distributed to the security's owners.

feasibility study A study to determine whether a proposed municipal project will generate sufficient funds to cover operation of the project and debt service. A feasibility study is generally required before the issuance of a municipal revenue bond.

federal funds The reserves of banks and certain other institutions greater than the reserve requirements; excess reserves. These funds are available immediately.

federal funds rate The interest rate charged by one institution lending federal funds to another.

Federal National Mortgage Association (FNMA, Fannie Mae) Purchases conventional mortgages and mortgages guaranteed by the Federal Housing Administration, Veterans Administration and Farmers Home Administration. FNMA is a publicly held corporation whose common stock is traded on the NYSE.

Federal Reserve Board (FRB) A seven-member group appointed by the President (subject to approval by Congress) to oversee operations of the Federal Reserve System.

Federal Reserve System (Fed) The central bank system of the United States. Its chief responsibility is to regulate the flow of money and credit.

final prospectus The prospectus delivered by an issuing corporation that includes the price of the securities, the delivery date, the underwriting spread and other material information.

Financial Guaranty Insurance Corporation (FGIC) An insurance company that offers insurance on the timely payment of interest and principal on municipal issues and unit investment trusts.

financial risk The risk associated with the safety of one's principal related to the ability of an issuer of a security to meet principal, interest or dividend payments.

fiscal policy The federal tax and spending policies set by Congress or the White House.

Fitch Investors Service, Inc. A rating service for corporate bonds, municipal bonds, commercial paper and other debt obligations.

fixed annuity (annuity guaranteed) An annuity contract in which the insurance company makes fixed dollar payments to the annuitant for the term of the contract (usually until the annuitant dies). The insurance company guarantees both earnings and principal amount. (*Syn.* fixed dollar annuity, guaranteed dollar annuity)

floor trader An exchange member who enters transactions only for a personal account from the floor of the exchange. (*Syn.* local)

foreign currency The currency of a country other than the one in which the investor resides. Options and futures contracts trade on numerous foreign currencies.

forward contract A cash market transaction in which a future delivery date is specified. Forward contracts differ from futures contracts in that the terms of forward contracts are not standardized and are not traded in contract markets.

fourth market The trading of securities directly from one institutional investor to another without the services of a brokerage firm.

fraud The deliberate concealment, misrepresentation or omission of material information or the truth to deceive or manipulate another party for unlawful or unfair gain.

freeriding and withholding A violation of the NASD Rules of Fair Practice, freeriding and withholding is the failure of a member participating in the distribution of a new issue to make a bona fide public offering at the public offering price for an issue that is hot. A hot issue is one that opens in the secondary market at a premium to the public offering price.

front-end load (1) The fees and expenses paid by any party for any service rendered during the program's organization or acquisition phase, including front-end organization and offering expenses, acquisition fees and expenses and any other similar fees designated by the sponsor. (2) A system of sales charge for contractual plans that permits up to 50% of the first year's payments to be deducted as a sales charge. Investors have a right to withdraw from the plan, but there are some restrictions if this occurs.

Full Disclosure Act Another name for the Securities Act of 1933.

fully registered A bond registered as to both principal and interest.

fund With mutual funds, the entity responsible for the general administration and supervision of the investment portfolio.

fundamental analysis A method of securities analysis that tries to evaluate the intrinsic value of a particular security. It is a study of the overall economy, industry conditions and the financial condition and management of a particular company.

fund manager With mutual funds, the entity responsible for investment advisory services.

futures Exchange-standardized contracts for the purchase or sale of a commodity at a future date.

futures contract A standardized, exchange-traded contract to make or take delivery of a particular type and grade of commodity at an agreed upon place and point in the future. Futures contracts are transferable between parties.

futures exchange A centralized facility for the trading of futures contracts.

futures market A continuous auction market in which participants buy and sell commodities contracts for delivery at a specified point in the future. Trading is carried on through open outcry and hand signals in a trading pit or ring.

general obligation bond (GO) A type of municipal bond backed by the full faith, credit and taxing power of the issuer for payment of interest and principal. (*Syn.* full faith and credit bond)

general partner (GP) A partner in a partnership who is personally liable for all debts of the partnership and who partakes in the management and control of the partnership.

general partnership (GP) An association of two or more entities forming to conduct a trade or partnership business. The partnership does not require documents for formation, and the general partners are jointly and severally liable for the partnership's liabilities.

Government National Mortgage Association (GNMA, Ginnie Mae) A wholly owned government corporation that issues several types of securities backed by the full faith and credit of the U.S. government.

government security An obligation of the U.S. government, backed by the full faith and credit of the government, and regarded as the highest grade or safest issue (i.e., default risk-free). The U.S. government issues short-term Treasury bills, medium-term Treasury notes and long-term Treasury bonds.

gross national product (GNP) The total value of goods and services produced in a society during one year. This includes consumption, government purchases, investment and exports minus imports.

growth fund A type of diversified common stock fund that has capital appreciation as its primary goal. It invests in companies that reinvest most of their earnings for expansion, research or develop-

ment. The term also refers to growth income funds that invest in common stocks for both current income and long-term growth of both capital and income.

growth stock A relatively speculative issue of a fast-growing company, often paying low dividends and selling at high price-earnings ratios.

hedge (1) The act of investing to reduce the risk of a position in a security (typically the risk of adverse price movements), normally by taking a protecting position in a related security. (2) The protective position taken.

high The highest price a security or commodity reaches during a specified period of time.

holding period A time period that starts the day after a purchase and ends on the day of the sale.

hot issue An issue that sells at a premium over the public offering price.

income fund A type of mutual fund that seeks to provide a stable current income from investments by investing in securities that pay interest.

Individual retirement account (IRA) A qualified tax-deferred retirement plan for employed individuals that allows a contribution of 100% of earned income up to a maximum of $2,000 per year. Some or all of the contribution may be tax deferred, depending on the individual's compensation level and coverage by other qualified retirement plans.

Inflation An increase in the general level of prices.

Initial margin requirement The amount of equity a customer must deposit when making a new purchase in a margin account. The Regulation T requirement is currently 50% for equity securities. The NYSE and NASD initial requirement is an equity of $2,000, but not more than 100% of the purchase cost.

Initial public offering (IPO) The first sale of stock by a company to the public (sometimes referred to as *going public*).

Insider Any person who has nonpublic knowledge (material information) about a corporation. Insiders include directors, officers and stockholders who own more than 10% of any class of equity security of a corporation.

INSTINET An electronic system owned by Reuters Holdings PLC that offers its subscribers a means of trading more than 10,000 U.S. and European securities without using a broker-dealer or going through an exchange. INSTINET collects price quotations from exchange-based market makers and NASDAQ and displays the best bid and asked for each security. INSTINET is registered as a broker-dealer with the SEC.

Institutional account An account held for the benefit of others. Examples of institutional accounts include banks, trusts, pension and profit-sharing plans, mutual funds and insurance companies. An institutional order can be of any size.

Institutional investor An organization that trades securities in large enough share quantities or dollar amounts that it qualifies for preferential treatment and lower trade costs (commissions). Institutional investors are covered by fewer protective regulations because it is assumed that they are more knowledgeable and better able to protect themselves.

In-the-money An option that has intrinsic value (e.g., a call option in which the stock is selling above the exercise price or a put option in which the stock is selling below the exercise price).

Intrastate offering A conditional offering of unregistered securities limited to companies that do business in one state and sell their securities only to residents of that same state (SEC Rule 147).

Intrinsic value The mathematical value of an option (e.g., a call option is said to have intrinsic value when the stock is trading above the exercise price).

Introducing broker A broker-dealer that does not hold investors' money or securities. Instead, it introduces those accounts to a clearing broker-dealer, which then handles all cash and securities for those accounts.

Investment adviser Any person who, for compensation (a flat fee or percentage of assets managed), offers investment advice. For investment companies, the adviser has the day-to-day responsibility of investing the cash and securities held in the mutual fund's portfolio. The adviser must adhere to the objectives as stated in the fund's prospectus. This definition includes persons who issue written reports or analyses for compensation.

Investment adviser representative Any partner, officer, director or other individual employed by or associated with an investment adviser who: (1) gives investment advice or makes recommendations, (2) manages client accounts or portfolios, (3) determines which investment recommendations or advice should be given, (4) offers or sells investment advisory services, or (5) supervises employees involved in any of these activities.

Investment banker A financial professional who raises capital for corporations and municipalities.

Investment banking (securities) business The business carried on by a broker, dealer or municipal or government securities dealer of underwriting or distributing new issues of securities as a dealer or of buying and selling securities on the order and for the benefit of others as a broker.

Investment company A company engaged primarily in the business of investing and trading in securities, including face-amount certificate companies, unit investment trusts and management companies.

Investment Company Amendments Act of 1970 Amendments to the Investment Company Act of 1940 requiring a registered investment company issuing periodic payment plan certificates (contractual plans) to offer all purchasers withdrawal rights and purchasers of front-end load plans surrender rights.

Investment Company Act Amendments of 1975 Amendments to the Investment Company Act of 1940; in particular, that sales charges must relate to the services a fund provides shareholders.

Investment Company Act of 1940 Congressional legislation enacted to regulate investment companies that requires any investment company in interstate commerce to register with the SEC.

Investment grade security A security with a rating (S&P, Moody's, etc.) of BBB/Baa or above.

Investment objective Any goal a client hopes to achieve through investing.

Investor The purchaser of a unit or security, including the sponsor to the extent that it purchases units.

IRA rollover The reinvestment of assets that an individual receives as a distribution from a qualified tax-deferred retirement plan into another qualified plan.

IRA transfer The direct movement and reinvestment of assets that an individual receives as a distribution from the custodian of one qualified tax-deferred retirement plan to the custodian of another qualified plan. IRA transfers differ from IRA rollovers in that in transfers the account owner never takes possession of the cash or securities received from the account, directing that the cash and securities be transferred directly from the existing plan custodian to the new plan custodian.

Issued stock Stock that has been sold to the public.

Issuer (1) The corporation or municipality that offers its securities for sale; also, the creator of an option (the issuer of an over-the-counter option is the option writer, and the issuer of a listed option is the Options Clearing Corporation). (2) According to the Uniform Securities Act, any person who issues or proposes to issue any security.

When a corporation or municipality raises additional capital through an offering of securities, that corporation or municipality is the "issuer" of those securities. An issuer transaction is also called a *primary transaction.*

Joint account An account in which two or more individuals act as cotenants or co-owners of the account. The account may be joint tenants in common or joint tenants with right of survivorship.

Joint tenants in common (JTIC) A form of ownership directing that upon the death of one tenant, the decedent's fractional interest in the joint account must be retained by the estate. This form of ownership may be used by any two or more individuals.

Joint tenants with right of survivorship (JTWROS) A form of ownership that requires that a deceased tenant's interest in an account be retained by the surviving tenant(s). It is often used by husbands and wives.

Keogh plan A qualified tax-deferred retirement plan for persons who are self-employed and unincorporated or who earn extra income through personal services

aside from their regular employment. (*Syn.* HR-10 plan)

L   L is a measure of the money supply that includes all of the components of M1, M2 and M3 as well as Treasury bills, savings bonds, commercial paper, bankers' acceptances and Eurodollar holdings of U.S. residents.

leverage The use of borrowed capital to increase earnings. (*Syn.* trading on the equity)

liability A debt owed by an entity; a legal obligation to pay. Current liabilities are debts payable within twelve months. Long-term liabilities are debts payable over a period of more than twelve months.

limited partner (LP) A partner who does not participate in the management or control of the partnership and whose liability for partnership debts is limited to the amount invested in the partnership.

limited partnership (LP) A form of business organization in which one or more of the partners are liable only to the extent of the amount of dollars they have invested. Limited partners are not involved in management decisions but enjoy direct flow-through of income and expenses.

limit order A customer's order with instructions to buy a specified security at or below a certain price or sell a specified security at or above a certain price. (*Syn.* or-better order)

liquidity The ease with which something can be bought or sold (converted to cash) in the marketplace. A large number of buyers and sellers and a high volume of trading activity are important components of liquidity.

listed option An option that can be bought and sold on a national securities exchange in a continuous secondary market. (*Syn.* standardized option)

listed security A security that is traded on a regional or national securities exchange such as the NYSE.

long The state of owning a security, contract or commodity. A purchase of 500 shares of AT&T would be referred to as *being long* AT&T. The investor would have a *long* position.

long market value (LMV) The current market price of the securities a customer owns, based on the closing prices of the previous day. (*Syn.* current market value)

low The lowest price a security or commodity reaches during a given period of time.

M1 A narrow definition of the money supply that includes only coins, currency, demand deposits (checking accounts) and NOW accounts.

M2 A broader definition of the money supply that includes coins, currency, demand deposits (checking accounts), time deposits, savings deposits and noninstitutional money-market funds.

M3 Those forms of money included in the M2 definition of the money supply plus large time deposits, institutional money-market funds, short-term repurchase agreements and certain other large liquid assets.

make a market The action of a broker-dealer firm when, on a regular basis, it holds itself out to other firms as ready to buy or sell a particular security for its own account. Such a firm accepts the risk of holding the position in the security.

Maloney Act Section 15 of the Securities Exchange Act of 1934 is known as the *Maloney Act*, named for its sponsor, the late Senator Francis Maloney of Connecticut. This legislation provided for the creation of the NASD, a securities industry association for the specific purpose of supervising the over-the-counter securities market.

margin The amount of equity as a percentage of current market value in a margin account.

margin account An account in which a brokerage firm lends a client part of the purchase price of securities.

margin call A demand for a client to deposit money or securities in a margin account.

margin department The department within a brokerage firm that computes the amount of money a client must deposit in both margin and cash accounts.

marketability The ease with which a security can be bought or sold; having a readily available market for trading.

market maker (principal) A dealer willing to accept the risk of holding securities to facilitate trading in a particular security or securities.

market order An order that is to be executed at the best price then available.

market risk That risk due to day-to-day fluctuations in prices at which securities can be bought or sold.

market value The price at which an investor will buy or sell each share of common stock or each bond at a given time; it is determined by the interaction between buyers and sellers in the market.

maturity date The date on which the principal is repaid to the investor.

member (1) Of the New York Stock Exchange (NYSE): One of the 1,366 individuals owning a seat on the NYSE. (2) Of the National Association of Securities Dealers (NASD): Any broker or dealer admitted to membership in the NASD. (3) Any broker or dealer admitted to membership of a regional exchange or another self-regulatory organization.

member firm A firm in which at least one of the principal officers is a member of the New York Stock Exchange, another organized exchange, a self-regulatory organization or a clearing corporation.

membership The members of the New York Stock Exchange, another exchange, a self-regulatory organization or a clearing corporation.

monetary policy The policies and actions of the Federal Reserve Board that determine the rate of growth and size of the money supply, which in turn affect interest rates.

money market The securities market that deals in short-term (less than one year) debt. Money-market instruments are forms of debt that mature in less than a year and are very liquid. Treasury bills make up the bulk of trading in the money markets.

money-market fund An open-end investment company investing in money-market instruments. Generally sold with no load, the fund offers draft-writing privileges and low opening investments.

municipal bond A debt security issued by a state, a municipality or another subdivision (such as a school, a park, or a sanitary or some other local taxing district) to raise money to finance its capital expenditures. Such expenditures might include the construction of highways, public works or school buildings.

municipal bond fund A type of mutual fund that invests in municipal bonds.

Municipal Bond Investors Assurance Corp. (MBIA) An insurance company offering insurance as to timely payment of principal and interest when due on qualified municipal issues. Most issues with MBIA insurance are rated AAA by Standard & Poor's and Moody's.

Munifacts A news wire service for the municipal bond industry; a product of *The Bond Buyer*.

mutual exclusion doctrine The doctrine that established the federal tax exemption status of municipal bond interest. This doctrine says that states and municipalities must not tax government-owned properties. The federal government reciprocates by excluding local government properties from federal taxation. (*Syn.* mutual reciprocity, reciprocal immunity)

mutual fund A type of investment company that offers for sale or has outstanding securities that it has issued that are redeemable on demand by the fund at current net asset value. All owners in the fund share in the gains or losses of the fund. (*Syn.* open-end management company)

mutual fund custodian Usually a national bank, a trust company or another qualified institution that physically safeguards securities. It does not manage investments; its function is solely clerical.

NASDAQ National Market System (NMS) The most actively traded over-the-counter stocks within the 4,000 stocks quoted on NASDAQ. Trades are reported as they occur.

NASDAQ 100 An index of the largest 100 nonfinancial stocks on NASDAQ weighted by capitalization.

NASD Automated Quotation System (NASDAQ) The nationwide electronic quotation system for up-to-the-minute bid and asked quotations on approximately 4,000 over-the-counter stocks.

NASD Bylaws The body of laws that describes how the NASD functions, defines its powers and determines the qualifications and registration requirements for brokers.

NASD District Business Conduct Committee (DBCC) A committee composed of up to twelve NASD members from within a district who serve as administrators for the district. The NASD is divided into 11 local districts to maximize the degree of local administration. The DBCC has original jurisdiction for hearings and judging complaints.

NASD Rules of Fair Practice In general, these rules complement and serve as extensions of the 1934 act rules and also the rules under the 1933 act and the Investment Company Act of 1940.

NASD Small Order Execution System (SOES) An automatic order execution system designed to facilitate the trading of small public market and executable limit orders (1,000 or fewer National Market System [NMS] shares; 500 or fewer non-NMS shares). Any NASDAQ or NASDAQ-NMS security with at least one active SOES market maker is eligible for trading through SOES.

SOES electronically matches and executes orders, locks in prices and sends confirms directly to the broker-dealers on both sides of the trades. Institutions and broker-dealers may not employ the system to trade for their own accounts. Only public market and executable limit orders are accepted by SOES.

National Association of Securities Dealers (NASD) The self-regulatory organization (SRO) for the over-the-counter (OTC) market. The NASD is generally recognized as the SRO for the OTC market.

National Futures Association (NFA) The self-regulatory organization of the commodities futures industry to which all futures exchange members, commodity-trading advisers (CTAs) and commodity pool operators (CPOs) must belong. The NFA is responsible to the Commodities Futures Trading Commission.

negotiable certificate of deposit (CD) A negotiable certificate that evidences a time deposit of funds with a bank. It is an unsecured promissory note normally issued in $100,000 denominations.

negotiated underwriting An underwriting in which a securities firm consults with the issuer and arrives at a consensus about the most suitable price and timing of a forthcoming securities offering.

net change The difference between the closing price on the trading day reported and the previous day's closing price. In many over-the-counter transactions, the term refers to the difference between the closing bids.

net worth The amount by which assets exceed liabilities. (*Syn.* shareholders' equity)

New Issues Act Another name for the Securities Act of 1933.

New York Stock Exchange (NYSE) A corporation operated by a board of directors responsible for setting policy, supervising Exchange and member activities, listing securities, overseeing the transfer of members' seats on the Exchange and judging whether an applicant is qualified to be a specialist.

no-load fund A mutual fund whose shares are sold without a sales charge added to the net asset value.

nominal yield The interest rate that is stated on the face of a bond representing the amount of interest paid by the issuer on the principal of the issue. (*Syn.* coupon rate, stated yield, yield)

noncumulative preferred stock A type of preferred stock that does not have to pay any dividends in arrears to the holders.

NYSE maintenance call A demand for a client to deposit money or securities if the client's equity falls below the NYSE minimum maintenance level.

NYSE maintenance requirement The minimum amount of equity that must be maintained in a margin account at all times according to NYSE rules. The minimum maintenance for all securities is 25% of the current market value for a long position.

NYSE Super Designated Order Turnaround system (SuperDot) The NYSE's computerized trading and execution system. Broker-dealers use this order routing system to choose the destination of an order and the route that order will take.

OCC Disclosure Document The disclosure document published by the Options Clearing Corporation that must be provided to every investor at the time the investor is approved for standardized options trading.

odd lot Less than the normal unit of trading, which generally means fewer than 100 shares of stock or five bonds.

odd lot order An order for less than the normal unit of trading (normally 100 shares of stock).

offer (1) An indication by an investor, a trader or a dealer of a willingness to sell a security or commodity. (2) Under the Uniform Securities Act, every attempt to solicit a purchase or sale in a security for value. (*Syn.* ask, quotation, quote)

offering circular A document that contains information about a corporation's issue of securities. The information included is similar to that made available in the prospectus but abbreviated. Its use is restricted to Regulation A offerings.

offering price With mutual funds, the price an investor will pay per share. The offering price is the net asset value plus a sales charge (for funds that have a sales charge). (*Syn.* current price)

official statement (OS) A statement concerning the municipal issue offered (disclosing the underwriting spread, fees received by brokers for acting as agents of the issuer and initial offering price of each maturity), prepared by the underwriter from information provided by the issuer.

oil and gas program A direct participation program that has as its primary purpose oil and gas exploration, development or purchase of production.

open-end management company A management company that continually issues new shares. Its shares are redeemable on any business day at the net asset value. Open-end management companies may sell only common stock. (*Syn.* mutual fund, open-end investment company)

open market operations The buying and selling of securities (primarily government or agency debt) by the Federal Open Market Committee for increasing or decreasing the level of bank reserves to effect control of the money supply.

option The right to buy (or sell) a specified amount of a security (stocks, bonds, futures contracts, etc.) at a specified price within a specified time. An option represents a right acquired by the purchaser, but it is an obligation only on the part of the option seller.

option agreement The agreement a customer must sign within 15 days of being approved for options trading. In it, the client agrees to abide by the rules of the listed options exchanges and not to exceed the exchanges' position or exercise limits.

Options Clearing Corporation (OCC) The organization through which the various options exchanges clear their trades. The OCC supervises the listing of new options and is considered the issuer of standardized options.

order department The department within a brokerage firm responsible for transmitting an order to the proper market for execution. (*Syn.* order room, wire room)

original issue discount (OID) A bond issued at a discount from face value at maturity. The bond may or may not pay interest, and the discount is taxed as if accrued annually as ordinary income. (*Syn.* stripped bond)

OTC Bulletin Board An electronic quotation system for non-NASDAQ securities; a computerized *Pink Sheet* for non-NASDAQ stock.

OTC option A put or call option that is not listed on an options exchange. All terms of the contract are negotiated between buyer and seller.

out-of-the-money A term referring to an option that has no intrinsic value (e.g., a put option in which the stock is selling above the exercise price or a call option in which the stock is selling below the exercise price).

outstanding stock Issued stock minus treasury stock (stock held by the issuing corporation); stock that is in the hands of the public.

over-the-counter (1) All securities markets other than the exchange markets are considered part of the over-the-counter market. (2) Any transaction that takes place in the over-the-counter market is considered an over-the-counter transaction.

Pacific Stock Exchange (PSE) SCOREX The PSE's Securities Communication, Order Routing and Execution (SCOREX) system, used to automatically route and execute orders. SCOREX serves the PSE as an automatic link between the national and regional stock exchanges, and quotes on SCOREX are based on quotes from each exchange trading that particular stock or option.

SCOREX accepts all types of orders, including market, good till canceled and limit orders in both odd and round lots. The specialists at the SCOREX terminals will execute orders up to the 10,099-share SCOREX limit and have the ability to waive that limit for larger orders.

paid-in capital That portion of shareholders' equity that has been generated through issuing stock above its stated value or through assets that have been received as gifts.

participating preferred stock A type of preferred stock that offers the holder a share of the earnings remaining after all senior securities have been paid. This payment is made in addition to the fixed dividend received. Dividends may be cumulative or noncumulative.

partnership A form of business organization in which two or more individuals manage the business and are equally and personally liable for its debts.

par value An arbitrary dollar value assigned to each share of stock at the time of issuance; the principal amount (face value) of a bond on which interest is calculated. (*Syn.* principal, stated value)

payment date The day on which a declared dividend is paid.

Philadelphia Stock Exchange (PHLX) PACE system The PHLX Automated Communication and Execution (PACE) system, developed by the PHLX in 1975 to automatically route and execute orders. PACE is designed to handle market and limit orders of up to 3,099 shares for more than 1,100 actively traded stocks.

PHLX Acronym for the Philadelphia Stock Exchange.

Pink Sheets The daily quotation sheets that publish the interdealer wholesale quotes for over-the-counter stocks.

position The amount of a security (shares, contracts, bonds, etc.) either owned (a long position) or owed (a short position) by an individual. A dealer will also take positions in specific securities to maintain an inventory to facilitate trading.

position trading (1) Occurs when a dealer acquires or sells an inventory in a security. (2) Occurs when a commodities speculator buys or sells positions in the futures markets as a means of speculating on long-term price movements.

preemptive right The legal right of stockholders to purchase new stock in proportion to their holdings before the new stock is offered to the public.

preferred stock An equity security that represents ownership in a corporation. Preferred stock has a fixed dividend, with dividend and asset preference over common stock, and it generally carries no voting rights.

preliminary prospectus Any prospectus that is distributed during the cooling-off period and includes the essential facts about the forthcoming offering except for the underwriting spread, final public offering price and date the shares will be delivered. (*Syn.* red herring)

premium The market price of an option; the cash price that the option buyer pays to the option writer; the price paid for a security over and above its face amount.

primary offering An offering in which the proceeds of the underwriting (either equity or debt) go to the issuing corporation or municipality. A corporation increases its capitalization by selling stock (either a new issue or a previously authorized but unissued stock). It may do this at any time and in any amount, provided the total stock outstanding never exceeds the amount authorized in the corporation's bylaws. A municipality raises money by issuing debt. (*Syn.* primary distribution)

prime rate The interest rate that commercial banks charge their prime or most creditworthy customers (generally large corporations).

principal (1) A person who positions trades in the secondary or primary market, including sole proprietors, officers, directors or partners of a company and managers of offices of supervision; also, an investment banker who assumes risk by actually buying securities from the issuer and reselling them. (*Syn.* dealer) (2) An arbitrary dollar value assigned to each share of stock at the time of issuance; the principal amount (face value) of a bond on which interest is calculated. (*Syn.* par value, stated value)

principal transaction A transaction where a broker-dealer buys stocks or bonds from customers and takes them into its own inventory. It then sells stocks or bonds to customers from its inventory.

prior preferred stock A class of preferred stock that has prior claim over other preferred stock in receipt of dividends, as well as in distribution of assets in the event of liquidation.

private placement An offering that complies with Regulation D (Rule 505 and Rule 506); generally speaking, the offer of an unregistered security to no more than 35 nonaccredited investors or to an unlimited number of accredited investors.

profitability The ability of a company to generate a level of income and gain in excess of expense.

program A limited or general partnership, a joint venture, an unincorporated association or a similar organization other than a corporation formed and operated for the primary purpose of investment in, operation of, or gain from an interest in real property, oil and gas property, or another suitable property.

proprietorship A business organization in which a single owner has total control over the business.

prospectus The legal document that must be given to every investor who purchases registered securities in an offering. It describes the details of the company and the particular offering. (*Syn.* final prospectus)

Prospectus Act Another name for the Securities Act of 1933.

proxy In order to vote on corporate matters, a stockholder must be represented at the annual meeting. If the stockholder is unable to attend, he may still vote by proxy. A proxy is given in writing, authorizing another to vote for the stockholder according to the stockholder's instructions.

PSE Acronym for the Pacific Stock Exchange.

Public Housing Authority bond (PHA) A bond issued by the Public Housing Authority. (*Syn.* Housing Authority bond)

public offering price (POP) The price of new shares that is established in the issuing corporation's prospectus; also, the price to investors for mutual fund shares.

purchases and sales department The department within a brokerage firm that computes the dollar amount of transactions, commissions and other charges, and sends confirmations to clients.

put (1) An option contract that gives the owner the right to sell a specified number of shares of stock at a specified price within a specified time. (2) The act of exercising a put option.

quotation The bid and ask of a particular security.

quote (bond) Like stock quotes, bond prices are quoted in the financial press and most daily newspapers. Corporate bonds are quoted in 1/8ths. Government bonds are quoted in 1/32nds. The quotes for corporate and government bonds are percentages of the bonds' face value ($1,000). Municipal bonds may be quoted on a dollar basis or on a yield to maturity.

quote (stock) Many stocks traded are quoted in the financial press and most daily newspapers. A stock is quoted in points, with each point equal to $1. The price of the stock is further broken down into 1/8ths of a point, where 1/8th equals 12.5 cents.

range A security's low price and high price for a particular trading period (e.g., close of the day's trading, opening of the day's trading, day, month, year). (*Syn.* opening range)

rating Bonds are rated for safety by various organizations such as Standard & Poor's and Moody's. These firms rate the companies and municipalities issuing bonds according to their ability to repay and make interest payments. Ratings range from AAA or Aaa (the highest) to C or D (representing a company in default).

rating service A company such as Moody's, Standard & Poor's, or Fitch that rates various debt and preferred stock issues for safety of payment of principal, interest or dividends. The issuing company or municipality pays a fee for the rating.

real estate investment trust (REIT) An investment trust that operates through the pooled capital of many investors who buy its shares. Investments are in the direct ownership of either income property or mortgage loans.

real estate program A direct participation program that has as its primary purpose the investment in or operation of real property for a gain.

record date The date established by the issuing corporation that determines which stockholders are entitled to receive dividends or rights distributions.

registered bond A bond on which the name of the owner appears on the certificate.

registered principal Anyone associated with a member who manages or supervises the member's

investment banking or securities business must be registered as a principal with the NASD. This includes those people involved in training associated persons and in soliciting business.

registered representative (RR) For NASD and NYSE registration and exam and licensing purposes: all associated persons engaged in the investment banking and securities business.

registered trader A member of an exchange who trades primarily for a personal account and at personal risk.

registrar An independent organization or part of a corporation charged with the responsibility of seeing that the corporation does not have more stock outstanding than is accounted for on the corporation's books.

registration statement Before nonexempt securities can be offered to the public, they require registration under the Securities Act of 1933. The registration statement must disclose all pertinent information concerning the issuer and the offering. This statement is submitted to the SEC in accordance with the requirements of the 1933 act.

regular way A settlement contract that calls for delivery and payment on the fifth business day following the date of trade. This is the usual type of settlement. For government securities, regular way is the next business day.

Regulation A The securities regulation that exempts small public offerings from registration (those valued at no more than $1.5 million worth of securities offered during a twelve-month period).

Regulation D The securities regulation that exempts from registration certain small offerings and sales to specified individuals during a twelve-month period.

Regulation G The Federal Reserve Board regulation governing the extension of credit by persons other than banks, brokers or dealers.

Regulation Q The Federal Reserve Board regulation that establishes how much interest banks may pay on savings accounts. Reg Q was phased out in 1986.

Regulation T The Federal Reserve Board regulation governing the credit that brokerage firms and dealers may extend to clients for the purchase of securities. Regulation T also governs cash accounts.

Regulation U The Federal Reserve Board regulation governing loans by banks for the purchase of securities. Call loans are exempt from Reg U.

repurchase agreement (repo) A sale and an attendant agreement to repurchase the securities sold at a higher price on an agreed upon future date. The difference between the sale price and the repurchase price represents the interest earned by the investor. In a repurchase agreement, the seller initiates the deal. Repos are commonly used by government securities dealers as a means of raising capital, typically to finance an inventory of securities. Repos are considered money-market instruments.

reserves The money that a bank has in its vault or on deposit with the Federal Reserve Bank. A bank is required to maintain a certain percentage of reserves as set by the Fed.

retail transaction A securities transaction for an individual rather than an institutional customer.

retained earnings The amount of net income that remains after all dividends have been paid to preferred and common stockholders. (*Syn.* earned surplus, reinvested earnings)

revenue bond A bond whose interest and principal are payable only from specific earnings of an income-producing (revenue-producing) enterprise; for example, a toll road.

reverse repurchase agreement (reverse repo) A purchase of securities and an attendant agreement to resell the securities at a higher price on an agreed upon future date. The difference between the purchase price and the sale price represents the interest earned by the investor. In a reverse repurchase agreement, the purchaser initiates the deal.

right A security representing a stockholder's right to purchase new securities in proportion to the number of shares already owned. Rights, also known as *stock rights*, are stock purchase options issued to existing stockholders only. The right is an option to purchase a company's new issue of stock at a predetermined price (normally for less than the stock's current market price). The right is issued for a short period of time, normally for 30 days, with the option expiring after that time. (*Syn.* subscription right certificate)

rights offering An offering that gives each stockholder an opportunity to maintain a proportionate ownership in the company when additional shares are offered to the public.

Rules of Fair Practice The NASD rules that detail how member firms deal with the public and with other members.

sales charge With mutual funds, the amount added to the net asset value (NAV) of mutual fund shares. The investor will pay the NAV and the sales charge, which equal the offering price. (*Syn.* sales load)

Securities Act of 1933 The federal legislation requiring the full and fair disclosure of all material information about the issuance of new securities.

Securities and Exchange Commission (SEC) The government agency created by Congress to protect investors. The Commission enforces the Securities Act of 1933, the Securities Exchange Act of 1934, the Trust Indenture Act of 1939, the Investment Company Act of 1940, the Investment Advisers Act of 1940, and others.

Securities Exchange Act of 1934 The federal legislation establishing the Securities and Exchange Commission. Its purpose is to provide regulation of securities exchanges and over-the-counter markets and to protect investors from unfair and inequitable practices.

Securities Industry Association (SIA) The nonprofit organization that represents the collective business interests of its more than 600 leading securities firm members headquartered throughout North America. SIA activities include government relations, industry research and a wide variety of educational, informational and other services for its members.

Securities Investor Protection Corporation (SIPC) A nonprofit membership corporation created by an act of Congress to protect clients of brokerage firms that are forced into bankruptcy. Membership is composed of brokers and dealers registered under the Securities Exchange Act of 1934 and engaged in public business, all members of national securities exchanges and most NASD members. SIPC provides customers of these firms up to $500,000 coverage for their cash and securities held by the firms (although coverage of cash is limited to $100,000).

security Under the act of 1934, any note, stock, bond, investment contract, debenture, certificate of interest in profit-sharing or partnership agreement, certificate of deposit, collateral trust certificate, preorganization certificate, option on a security or another instrument of investment commonly known as a "security."

self-regulatory organization (SRO) Each SRO is accountable to the SEC for the enforcement of federal securities laws, as well as the supervision of securities practices, within an assigned field of jurisdiction. Eight SROs function under the oversight of the Commission. Selected jurisdictions include:

- New York Stock Exchange (NYSE). All matters related to trading in NYSE-listed securities and the conduct of NYSE member firms and associated persons.
- National Association of Securities Dealers (NASD). All matters related to investment banking (securities underwriting) and trading in the over-the-counter market and the conduct of NASD member firms and associated persons.
- Municipal Securities Rulemaking Board (MSRB). All matters related to the underwriting and trading of state and municipal securities.
- Chicago Board Options Exchange (CBOE). All matters related to the writing and trading of standardized options and related contracts listed on that exchange.

sell Along with "sale," refers to any contract to sell a security or an interest in a security.

Series EE bond A nonmarketable U.S. government savings bond issued at a discount from par.

Series HH bond A nonmarketable interest-bearing U.S. government savings bond issued at par.

settlement The completion of a securities trade through the delivery of the security (or commodity) for cash or another consideration.

settlement date The date on which a transaction must be settled (exchange of cash for securities).

shareholders' equity Calculated by subtracting total liabilities

from total assets. (*Syn.* net worth, owners' equity)

short The state of having sold a security, contract or commodity. A sale of 10 September silver contracts would be referred to as *going short*, or *shorting*, September silver. The speculator would have a *short* position.

short sale The sale of a security that the seller does not own or any sale consummated by the delivery of a security borrowed by or for the account of the seller.

sole proprietorship A form of business organization in which a single owner has total control over the business.

specialized fund A type of mutual fund that tries to achieve its investment objectives by concentrating its investments within a single industry or group of related industries.

special situation fund A type of mutual fund that invests in companies in special situations, such as firms undergoing reorganization or firms considered to be takeover candidates.

speculation The buying and selling of goods or securities with high risk solely for the purpose of profiting from those trades and not as a means of hedging or protecting other positions.

sponsor Any person directly or indirectly instrumental in organizing, wholly or in part, a partnership; or any person who will manage or participate in the management of a partnership.

Standard & Poor's 500 A market indicator composed of 400 industrial stocks, 20 transportation stocks, 40 financial stocks and 40 public utility stocks.

statutory disqualification A person is statutorily disqualified from association with a member organization if that person has been expelled, barred or suspended from association with a member of a self-regulatory organization; has had a registration suspended, denied or revoked by the SEC; has been the cause of someone else's suspension, barment or revocation; has been convicted of certain specified crimes; or has falsified any application or report that is required to be filed with or on behalf of a membership organization.

stock certificate Written evidence of ownership in a corporation.

Stock Market Game™ A simulation in which teams of students compete against one another as they invest a hypothetical $100,000. Hundreds of thousands of students and teachers across the United States participate annually in the Stock Market Game (SMG), which is designed to foster a better understanding of the nation's economic system. SMG is sponsored by the Securities Industry Association.

strike price The price at which the underlying security will be sold if the option buyer exercises her rights in the contract. (*Syn.* exercise price)

strip bond A bond stripped of its coupons, repackaged and sold at a deep discount, and maturing at full face value.

syndicate A group of broker-dealers formed to handle the distribution and sale of an issuer's security. The typical syndicate has one or more firms managing the underwriting effort. Each member of the syndicate is then assigned responsibility for the sale and distribution of a portion of the issue.

technical analysis A method of securities analysis that analyzes statistics generated by market activity, such as past prices and volume. Technical analysis does not attempt to measure a security's intrinsic value.

third market The trading of listed securities in the over-the-counter market by nonexchange members.

trade confirmation A bill or comparison of a trade that is sent to a customer on or before the first day of business following the trade date.

trade date The date on which a transaction occurs.

transfer agent A person or an organization responsible for recording the names of registered stockholders and the number of shares owned, seeing that the certificates are signed by the appropriate corporate officers, affixing the corporate seal and delivering the securities to the transferee.

Treasury bill A marketable, short-term (90 days to one year) U.S. government debt security issued through a competitive bidding process at a discount from par value. There is no fixed interest rate.

Treasury bond A marketable, long-term (10 to 30 years), fixed-interest U.S. government debt security.

Treasury note A marketable, medium-term (one to ten years), fixed-interest U.S. government debt security.

trust indenture The written agreement between a corporation and its creditors that details the terms of the debt issue. These terms include such things as the rate of interest, the maturity date, the means of payment and the collateral. (*Syn.* deed of trust, trust agreement)

Trust Indenture Act of 1939 The legislation requiring that all publicly offered, nonexempt debt securities be registered under the Securities Act of 1933 and issued under a trust indenture.

Trust in Securities Act Another name for the Securities Act of 1933.

12b-1 asset-based fees Under Section 12b-1 of the Investment Company Act of 1940, the fees that a company may collect for the promotion, sale or other activity connected with the distribution of its shares; such fees are determined annually either as a flat dollar amount or as a percentage of the company's average total net asset value during the year.

two-dollar broker A member of an exchange who freelances by executing orders for various member firms when their own floor brokers are especially busy. The broker charges a commission for her services. The amount of the commission is negotiated, though at one time $2 was the standard charge for a round lot.

underlying securities The futures or securities that are bought or sold when an option is exercised, or those on which an option is based.

underwriter The entity responsible for marketing stocks, bonds, mutual fund shares and so on.

underwriting The procedure by which investment bankers channel investment capital from investors to corporations and municipalities.

underwriting manager The brokerage firm responsible for organizing a syndicate, preparing the issue, negotiating with the issuer and underwriters and allocating stock to the selling group. (*Syn.* manager, manager of the syndicate, managing underwriter)

underwriting syndicate A group of brokerage firms that agree in writing to cooperate in a joint venture to distribute a particular offering of securities. (*Syn.* syndicate)

Uniform Gifts to Minors Act (UGMA) The act that permits gifts of money and securities to be given to minors and allows adults to act as custodians for minors.

Uniform Practice Code The NASD code that governs and makes uniform a firm's dealings with other brokerage firms.

unit investment trust (UIT) An investment company that has its own portfolio of securities in which it invests. It sells interests in this portfolio in the form of redeemable securities. UITs can be of two types: fixed (no portfolio changes can be made) and nonfixed (portfolio changes are permissible). Unit investment trusts are organized under a trust indenture, not a corporate charter.

variable annuity A form of annuity issued by life insurance companies. Like fixed annuities, variable annuities guarantee payment for life once the contract is annuitized, and the issuing insurance company accepts the mortality risk for the client. However, unlike fixed annuities, the variable annuity contract does not guarantee the amount of the annuity payment or performance of the account in that both will vary according to the performance of the securities or other assets in which the funds are invested. The annuitant, not the company, accepts the investment risk.

volatility The speed with which and the extent to which the price of a security or commodity rises and falls within a given period of time.

Wall Street (1) The financial district in downtown New York City. (2) A blanket term applied to the U.S. securities and investment industry, regardless of location.

warrant A security giving the holder the right to purchase securities at a stipulated price. This is usually a long-term instrument, affording the investor the option of buying shares at a later date at the subscription price, subject to the warrant's exercise.

wholesale transaction A trade in which a broker-dealer buys an over-the-counter stock from another broker-dealer.

writer The seller of an option. (*Syn.* guarantor, holder, seller)

Yellow Sheets Pages that the National Quotation Bureau publishes daily and that contain wholesale quotations of dealers for corporate bonds.

yield The rate of return on an investment, generally expressed as a percentage of the current price. (*Syn.* current yield, dividend yield)

Index